LIGHT SHINES

100 meditations for Lent

NICK FAWCETT

kevin mayhew

kevin
mayhew

First published in Great Britain in 2011 by Kevin Mayhew Ltd
Buxhall, Stowmarket, Suffolk IP14 3BW
Tel: +44 (0) 1449 737978 Fax: +44 (0) 1449 737834
E-mail: info@kevinmayhewltd.com

www.kevinmayhew.com

9 8 7 6 5 4 3 2 1 0

ISBN 978 1 84867 399 1

Catalogue No. 1501287

Cover design by Rob Mortonson
© Image used under licence from Shutterstock Inc.

Project managed by Free Range Book Design & Production

Printed and bound in Great Britain

Contents

Costly commitment

Examining ourselves

Faith and works

Time and space for God

New beginnings

Jesus transfigured

Mothering Sunday

About the author

Nick Fawcett trained for the Baptist ministry at Bristol and Oxford, before going on to serve in pastorates in Leigh, Lancashire, and Gas Green, Cheltenham. He subsequently spent three years as a chaplain with the Christian movement Toc H, before deciding the time was right to commit himself to a writing ministry, supplementing his income through freelance editing. He has written over a hundred and twenty books, many of which have sold thousands of copies.

Together with their two children, Samuel and Kate, he lives with his wife, Deborah, in Wellington, Somerset, worshipping at the local Anglican church. A keen walker, gardener and chess player, as well as supporter of Southend United and local team Tiverton Town, Nick delights in the beauty of the Somerset and Devon countryside around his home, his numerous books owing much to the inspiration he unfailingly finds there.

Introduction

Those familiar with my writing will know what great store I set on using meditations to explore the meaning of Scripture. My interest in this medium began at a Good Friday service many years ago, built around reflective material written by various authors. Never having encountered such an approach before, I was spellbound, fascinated by the way familiar passages of Scripture and events from the life of Jesus suddenly spoke to me with new and unexpected power. This, I resolved, was a means of communication I needed to include in my own ministry. But when I looked for similar material covering other seasons of the Christian year or the wider message of the gospel, I struggled to find much that seemed suitable, to the point that I decided eventually the only solution was to write some myself. The opportunity came during a sabbatical, kindly allowed me by Gas Green Baptist Church during my time as minister there. In ten weeks I wrote a hundred meditations, subsequently published by Kevin Mayhew as my first book, *No Ordinary Man*, and since then I've produced a host of other books, many of which likewise use meditations to reflect on Scripture, life and faith.

In this book – one of a series for seasons of the Christian year – I've put together revised material from eight publications – *Decisions, Decisions, To Put It Another Way, The Unfolding Story, No Ordinary Man 1* and 2, and three volumes of *A Most Amazing Man* – to compile a comprehensive reflective resource for Lent. The meditations – some linked to the Bible readings recommended in *Common Worship*, others to passages documenting other incidents in the life and ministry of Jesus – are each rounded off by a short prayer on the theme.

How you use the book is, of course, entirely up to you. You may employ a single meditation alongside a sermon to reinforce its message, or perhaps even in place of the sermon altogether – say in a family service of some experimental act of worship. Alternatively, you may want to use several meditations to create a reflective service of your own aimed at presenting the message of one of these familiar seasons in a novel and arresting way. Or, of course, you may simply have bought this book as a tool for personal devotion. However you use it, my hope is that will help to bring new meaning into this season of prayer, reflection and rededication; new insights into God's love so wonderfully revealed in Christ.

Nick Fawcett

Testing and temptation

1

Was I tempted?

Joseph, son of Jacob

Now Joseph was handsome and good-looking. And after a time his master's wife cast her eyes on Joseph and said, 'Lie with me.' But he refused. And although she spoke to Joseph day after day, he would not consent to lie beside her or to be with her. One day, however, when he went into the house to do his work, and while no one else was in the house, she caught hold of his garment, saying, 'Lie with me!' But he left his garment in her hand, and fled and ran outside. Then she kept his garment by her until his master came home, and she told him the same story, saying, 'The Hebrew servant, whom you have brought among us, came in to me to insult me; but as soon as I raised my voice and cried out, he left his garment beside me, and fled outside.' When his master heard the words that his wife spoke to him, saying, 'This is the way your servant treated me,' he became enraged. And Joseph's master took him and put him into the prison, the place where the king's prisoners were confined; he remained there in prison.

Genesis 39:6b–8a, 10–12, 16–20

Meditation

Was I tempted?
You bet I was!
She was an attractive woman, let's face it,
suave, sophisticated, sexy,
and I was a young man in my prime,
flattered and excited by her attentions.
My pulse raced when she looked at me,
palms sweating,
body crying out to surrender,
but I couldn't, for both our sakes,
not just mine.
Oh, I'd have enjoyed it, no doubt –
for a moment, in the heat of passion,
nothing else would have seemed to matter;
but then the guilt would have started,

the regrets,
the sordid subterfuge,
and finally, punishment!
She was married, you see,
my master's wife,
and the vows she'd taken were sacred,
whichever god she'd made them by.
So I refused her, time and again,
keeping my distance whenever I could.
Only she wouldn't take no for an answer,
waiting patiently to seize her chance.
I should have it seen it coming, I suppose,
for I knew she was put out –
you could see that a mile off –
unused, apparently, to being turned down,
but I never thought she'd come on that strong,
not after all I'd said.
It was a close call eventually,
too close for comfort,
costing me my clothes, if not my virtue.
But it wasn't just my robe I lost that day;
it was my freedom, position and reputation,
for she turned the tables as I knew she would,
making *me* out to be the guilty party –
'hell hath no fury . . .' as they say.
Whatever I lost though, I kept far more,
my integrity,
my self-respect,
and, above all, my faith.
A price worth paying, wouldn't you say?

Prayer

Loving God,
you know what it is to be tempted,
for you took on human flesh,
making yourself frail and vulnerable, just as we are.
You know what it is to lose everything,
for you gave your only Son for the life of the world.
For our sakes you became poor,
enduring humiliation,

yet you stood firm,
refusing to be swayed or to contemplate compromise.
Teach us, in our turn, to hold fast, come what may.
When temptation comes,
help us to look to you rather than self,
to *your* kingdom rather than *our* gratification.
Show us the way you would have us take,
and help us to walk it faithfully.
Amen.

2

What was he doing, going off into the wilderness like that?

John the Baptist

And the Spirit immediately drove him out into the wilderness. He was in the wilderness for forty days, tempted by Satan; and he was with the wild beasts; and the angels waited on him. Now after John was arrested, Jesus came to Galilee, proclaiming the good news of God, and saying, 'The time is fulfilled, and the kingdom of God has come near; repent, and believe in the good news.'

Mark 1:12–15

Meditation

What was he doing, going off into the wilderness like that?
I'd baptised him just moments earlier,
seen God's blessing rest upon him –
confirmation, if any were needed, that he was the one sent from God,
the Messiah for whom we longed –
and I'd expected him to hit the ground running:
to rally support,
energise the crowds,
lay claim at once to his throne.
But instead, he disappeared,
heading off into the hills,
and no sight or sound of him for weeks to come.
Was he having second thoughts, I wondered?
Was the job too much for him?
Or had I simply misunderstood my man?
I watched . . .
and I waited . . .
torn between a mixture of dread and hope,
until, at last, word came that he was healing the sick,
saving the lost,
proclaiming the dawn of God's kingdom.
Suddenly I understood.

He'd needed to experience the wasteland of temptation
before he was ready to transform the desert of human life.
He'd faced the stark choice of self or others,
of taking the easy or hard way,
and he'd resolved to give his all.
Quite simply, but wonderfully,
he'd entered the wilderness to lead us out!

Prayer

Lord Jesus Christ,
when we wrestle with temptation,
struggling to overcome the inner voice that seeks to lead us astray,
remind us that we are not left to face it alone.
When we *fall* to temptation,
giving in yet again to what we know to be wrong,
compromising our convictions,
denying your love,
betraying our calling,
remind us that you understand.
When we despair of ourselves,
frustrated at our weakness,
our lack of faith,
our fragile commitment
and our feeble resolve,
remind us that we are not forgotten.
Teach us that you too faced temptation,
and overcame it;
that you turned your back on the rewards of this world
so that we might rejoice in the riches of your kingdom.
Help us to receive your generous forgiveness
and to walk your way more faithfully,
not in *our* strength,
but in *yours*.
Amen.

3

I thought I had him

The devil

Jesus, full of the Holy Spirit, returned from the Jordan and was led by the Spirit in the wilderness, where for forty days he was tempted by the devil.

Luke 4:1, 2a

Meditation

I thought I had him.
Not just once but three times I thought I'd caught him out.
And I was close,
even *he*, I expect, would give me that.
Oh, he seemed confident enough when he first arrived in the wilderness –
sure of his destiny and his ability to grasp it.
But then he would have done, wouldn't he,
coming straight after his baptism,
heart still skipping within him,
the memory fresh,
the voice of God ringing in his ears?
But forty days on –
forty days of gnawing hunger, desert heat and night-time chill –
it was a different story,
hard then to think of anything but the pain in his belly
and the simple comforts of home.
So I saw my chance,
and made my move.
Nothing crude or clumsy –
no point scaring him off unnecessarily –
just a subtle whisper,
a sly suggestion:
'Turn this stone into bread.'
And he was tempted, don't be fooled.
I could see by the gleam in his eyes and the way he licked his lips
that, if you'll pardon the expression, he was chewing it over.
It wouldn't have taken much to make him crack, I'm certain of it;

one whiff of a fresh-baked loaf
and I'm sure he'd have given in –
why didn't I think of it!
Only then he remembered those cursed Scriptures of his –
'One does not live by bread alone' –
and all my hard work was undone in a moment.
It was a setback,
but I pressed on, confident I was making ground.
And, soon after, he was up on the mountains,
the world stretching out before him as far as the eye could see.
'All this is yours!' I whispered.
'Just forget this Messiah business and grab it while you can.'
Oh, you may sneer with hindsight at my methods,
but it's worked before,
many a lofty ideal sacrificed on the altar of ambition.
But not Jesus –
in fact, this time not even a suggestion of compromise:
'It is written, "Worship the Lord your God, and serve only him."'
So I took him in his imagination up on to the Temple
and played my trump card:
'Go on,' I urged him, 'Throw yourself off.
If you are who you think you are, God will save you,
for *it is written*:
"He will command his angels concerning you, to protect you."'
A master-stroke, so I thought,
quoting his own Scriptures at him like that,
and, let's face it, we all like a little reassurance, don't we,
however strong our faith;
the knowledge, should the worst come to the worst,
that there'll be someone to bail us out when we need them?
'Why should he be any different?' I reasoned –
he was as human as the next man,
as vulnerable as the rest of your miserable kind.
But, somehow, even then he held firm:
'It is said,' he answered, '"Do not put the Lord your God to the test."'
Well, that was it,
I knew I was beaten.
There was nothing left to throw at him,
so I slithered away to lick my wounds.
But I'll be back, you mark my words,
and next time, when it's his very life in the balance,

a question of do or die,
then we'll see what he's really made of, won't we?
Then we'll see which of us is finally the stronger.

Prayer

Lord of all,
we are reminded today that even Jesus faced temptation:
the temptation to compromise his convictions,
abandon his calling,
serve himself rather than others.
Teach us to recognise the many similar temptations *we* face in turn,
some easy to spot
but others so subtle that we give in to them without realising it.
Give us a clear sense of what you would have us do
and all you would have us be,
and grant us the courage and commitment we need
to stand firm whenever temptation strikes,
offering you true and faithful service.
Amen.

4

'Go on,' I told him

The devil

Then the devil took him to Jerusalem, and placed him on the pinnacle of the temple, saying to him, 'If you are the Son of God, throw yourself down from here, for it is written, "He will command his angels concerning you, to protect you", and "On their hands they will bear you up, so that you will not dash your foot against a stone."' Jesus answered him, 'It is said, "Do not put the Lord your God to the test."'

Matthew 4:9–12

Meditation

'Go on,' I told him,
'throw yourself off!
God's angels will save you –
you know it's true.'
And for a wonderful moment I actually thought it might work –
my efforts succeed at last.
All right, so I'd tried twice already,
appealing first to hunger,
then to greed,
but those were bodged attempts,
crude and clumsy,
destined to fail from the start.
This time I'd learnt from my mistakes
got the measure of my man,
and was ready to pounce.
You see, it wasn't plenty he was after,
or power,
or any form of personal gain,
but to serve *God*,
putting *him* first and self second,
the good of others before his own –
and, disturbingly, he was serious,
resolved to stay true whatever the cost.

I knew he could do it,
but did *he*? –
that was the question.
He was human, remember,
as prone as the rest of you to that niggling voice of doubt,
and who better than *me* to oblige!
'So you're God's Son,' I murmured.
'Yes, of course.
'But why not be sure?
'Why lean on faith when proof is in your grasp?'
And then, to clinch it all,
a whispered aside:
'God doesn't want you to die.'
Only of course, God *did*,
and somehow, even then, Jesus understood,
ready to take him on trust and give his all.
Well, that was it,
no point trying any more,
for if *that* wouldn't crack him,
nothing would.
He'd resisted temptation,
refusing to yield,
and, to cap it all,
as I sloped off, those angels I'd promised appeared by his side,
not to *save* him,
but to help him stay true,
so that, far from *cheating* death,
he would *beat* it,
once and for all.

Prayer

Lord Jesus Christ,
we praise you for walking the way of the cross;
for standing firm to the end,
refusing to compromise your calling,
instead of succumbing to the temptation to put yourself first.
Forgive our weakness that stands in such contrast to your strength –
the ease with which we are led astray,
the readiness with which we dilute our principles,
the excuses with which we shut out your voice,

preferring instead, our own.
Help us to follow you more faithfully,
not in any attempt to earn your love but simply to respond to it,
celebrating the grace that reconciles us to you,
despite all that keeps us apart.
Amen.

5

I gave up eventually

The devil

When the devil had finished every test, he departed from him until an opportune time.

Luke 4:13

Meditation

I gave up eventually,
for it was futile to continue,
all my efforts a waste of time.
Try as I might,
I was never going to deflect this guy from the straight and narrow,
even if I stayed out there in the desert for ever.
I'd deployed my usual tricks –
the promise of material comfort,
earthly glory,
divine protection –
and each time he'd seen through me,
committing himself yet more firmly to his chosen path.
So I made my exit,
discretion being the better part of valour and all that.
But don't imagine for a moment I'd finished with him.
Not likely!
You might have given up, perhaps,
but not me –
it's simply not my style to lose heart at the first setback.
No,
mine was more of a tactical retreat,
a temporary withdrawal to consider options,
make fresh plans,
before coming at him again.
And mark my words,
there would be opportunities,
for you humans, even one as unusual as him,

all have your weak spots,
places where I can prod and probe until you finally succumb.
You think he's different?
Well, we'll see about that.
Let's wait till he's asked to choose between survival and surrender,
between looking after number one
and pursuing his ridiculous way of love and service to the bitter end.
Then we'll see what he's made of, won't we?
Then we'll know, one way or the other,
which of us is the stronger.

Prayer

Lord Jesus Christ,
you know what it is to be tempted, just as we are,
yet, such was the closeness of your relationship with God,
that you always stood firm,
resisting whatever would deflect you from your calling.
Give us strength to withstand temptation in turn,
to say no to the siren voices that seek to lead us astray.
Help us so to know you that we delight to walk your way,
and when we wander from your side,
through your grace draw us back.
Amen.

6

He looked awful

Mary, mother of Jesus

Then Jesus, filled with the power of the Spirit, returned to Galilee, and a report about him spread through all the surrounding country.

Luke 4:14

Meditation

He looked awful,
absolutely drained.
And it's hardly surprising, is it?
Forty days out in the wilderness is hell enough for anyone,
but without food – I ask you?
He was lucky to be alive!
Barely was, mind you, when he came staggering back into Nazareth,
gaunt and starving!
'Why did you do it?' I asked him.
'What got into you?'
And all he could say was that he *had* to,
that everything depended on it.
He was changed afterwards.
I used to joke that the sun had got to him.
But it wasn't the sun, of course,
It was much more than that.
He wrestled out there,
with himself,
with the world,
with all the forces of evil,
and in some way I don't quite understand,
he won.
It had cost him, though.
He'd had to make painful choices,
confronting life at its darkest
and wrestling with who he was and why he was here.
But he came back stronger,

more certain and determined.
Not that it was plain sailing from then on,
don't make that mistake.
He had to battle like you and I,
harder if anything,
for the path he took was so much more demanding.
Oh no, he endured temptation all right,
as real as any we might face.
The difference is, he overcame it,
right to the end.
That's what made him so special.
That's why people follow him, even now!

Prayer

Gracious God,
we thank you for the time spent by Jesus in the wilderness,
tested there to the limit but refusing to be deceived.
Help us to learn from his example;
to be awake to temptation and ready to withstand it;
to make time to hear your voice and reflect upon your word.
Help us to grow closer to you and stronger in faith,
so that we may follow you and do your will,
regardless of the cost.
Amen.

7

Don't be too hard on me

Demas

Do your best to come to me soon, for Demas, in love with this present world, has deserted me and gone to Thessalonica.

2 Timothy 4:9, 10a

Meditation

Don't be too hard on me.
I know I've failed, all too well.
I don't need anyone to twist the knife,
for I do that myself every day.
Demas, the man who fell away,
that's what they'll call me;
the man who couldn't stay the course,
who found the going too tough.
I can see it all now –
they'll preach sermons about me,
warning against falling away,
turning back;
and though none of them will know just why it happened,
they'll make their guesses,
a multitude of suggestions in the quest to safeguard souls.
Cowardice,
doubt,
weakness,
ambition –
plenty to choose from –
and yes, it's true, each played a part.
I *was* afraid of the cost,
terrified at the thought of pain,
the prospect of death.
I *did have* my doubts,
many of them,
all sorts of questions unresolved.

Weak?
Of course I was –
careless in devotion,
feeble in self-discipline,
too easily led astray.
And ambitious?
Certainly.
I was eager to get on in the world,
anxious to keep in with the right people
and afraid that being associated with Jesus might give the wrong idea.
But if that was true of me it was true of others also,
yet *they* still follow,
so why not me?
I wish I knew,
I really do,
but somehow the magic's gone,
the sparkle that made faith come alive.
And though I could pretend it's there,
put on a front and claim I still believe,
I ask you, what would be the point?
I might deceive others,
perhaps in time even fool myself,
but not Jesus,
not him.
I know I've failed,
he knows I've failed,
and I can only pray that he will accept me now
as he accepted me then,
despite myself.

Prayer

Living God,
we pray for those who find faith hard,
those who want to believe but cannot get past their doubts.
We pray for those whose faith is wavering,
undermined by the pressures and temptations of life.
We pray for those who have lost their faith,
the fire that once burned within them extinguished.

And we pray for ourselves,
conscious that for us, also, faith can all too easily lose its spark.
For ourselves and all facing the dark night of faith,
we pray: 'I do believe, help thou my unbelief.'
Amen.

Grace and mercy

8

Was it a punishment for those mistakes long ago?

Jacob

Then Judah said to his brothers, 'What profit is it if we kill our brother and conceal his blood? Come, let us sell him to the Ishmaelites, and not lay our hands on him, for he is our brother, our own flesh.' And his brothers agreed. When some Midianite traders passed by, they drew Joseph up, lifting him up out of the pit, and sold him to the Ishmaelites for twenty pieces of silver. And they took Joseph to Egypt. Then they took Joseph's robe, slaughtered a goat, and dipped the robe in the blood. They had the long robe with sleeves taken to their father, and they said, 'This we have found; see now whether it is your son's robe or not.' He recognised it, and said, 'It is my son's robe! A wild animal has devoured him; Joseph is without doubt torn to pieces.' Then Jacob tore his garments, and put sackcloth on his loins, and mourned for his son many days. All his sons and all his daughters sought to comfort him; but he refused to be comforted, and said, 'No, I shall go down to Sheol to my son, mourning.'

Genesis 37:26–28, 31–35

Meditation

Was it a punishment for those mistakes long ago,
God paying me back for having cheated and connived
to make his blessing mine?
I thought so at the time when my boys came back –
all bar Joseph –
tears streaming down their faces,
wringing their hands in sorrow.
I believed the worst at once,
heart lurching within me.
Call me gullible, if you like,
but what reason did I have to doubt their word?
They produced his robe, remember,
dripping in blood,
ripped to shreds,

and I assumed immediately he'd been torn to pieces,
my precious boy set upon by a wild beast.
All right, so they'd had their disagreements,
even come to blows occasionally,
but which boys don't? –
it's part of growing up.
They must have known he was harmless,
despite those crazy dreams of his;
conceited, perhaps,
but innocent enough beneath it all.
I never dreamt for a moment they hated him,
still less that they might do him in,
so when they broke the news that he was dead
I accepted it without question –
shattered,
inconsolable,
yet convinced it was true.
Divine judgement, it seemed, had come at last.
Only it wasn't God I should have blamed,
nor my sons, come to that –
it was me,
for I was the cause of it all.
I spoiled him, you see, that lad of mine, from the day he was born,
thrusting him forward,
pandering to his whims,
not just accepting his airs and graces but positively encouraging them.
I should have learnt from the past,
remembered the heartache my mum's favouring of *me* had caused.
But I was blind,
and the wheel turned full circle.
I couldn't have complained had the lad been dead,
for I deserved punishment after everything I'd done,
no sentence too severe.
Yet God was gracious.
his hand upon Joseph,
upon us all,
and I realise now that though the past *did* catch up with me that day,
God was already leading me forward into his future!

Prayer

Lord,
we find it hard to escape from the past.
It has shaped our lives in so many ways,
helping to make us what we are today.
And though there have been successes,
there have been mistakes also that continue to haunt us.
We find it hard to let go of regrets,
to put past failures behind us and start again.
Yet you are the God who holds the future,
always ready to forget what has been
and lead us on to what shall be;
a God of new beginnings, new hope, new life.
Help us to grasp the full implications of what that means,
and, accepting each day you give us,
to live it to the full,
assured of your unfailing love.
Amen.

9

I met him out on the hills

David

The Lord is my shepherd, I shall not want. He makes me lie down in green pastures; he leads me beside still waters; he restores my soul. He leads me in right paths for his name's sake. Even though I walk through the darkest valley, I fear no evil; for you are with me; your rod and your staff – they comfort me. You prepare a table before me in the presence of my enemies; you anoint my head with oil; my cup overflows. Surely goodness and mercy shall follow me all the days of my life, and I shall dwell in the house of the Lord my whole life long.

Psalm 23:1–6

Meditation

I met him out on the hills –
a solitary shepherd,
brow furrowed,
searching for a sheep gone astray.
And suddenly it all came flooding back,
those long hours I had spent as a boy
out in the fields tending my father's flock.
Good days, on the whole –
time to think,
pray,
or simply enjoy the beauty of this world God has given.
But demanding also,
even dangerous sometimes –
out in the fiercest of storms,
harassed by wild beasts,
keeping watch through the lonely hours of the night.
Funny really, isn't it? –
all that over a bunch of sheep,
for let's face it, they're stupid creatures at the best of times,
often driving you to distraction.
You try to help them, and what do they do?

Wander away as soon as look at you,
straight into the teeth of some new danger.
Infuriating!
Yet somehow a bond develops,
until the time comes when, if you're worth your salt,
you'll do anything for those sheep,
even risk your own life to save their necks.
We're like sheep ourselves in a way,
as foolish, headstrong and maddening as any of them –
following the crowd,
ignoring guidance,
careering blindly towards catastrophe.
Why should anyone bother with us?
And yet the Lord does just that,
like a shepherd, always being there to guard us, guide us, feed us,
seeking when we're lost,
rejoicing when we're found,
protecting us from evil.
Would he risk his life for us, as I for my sheep?
It sounds ridiculous, I know,
too fanciful for words,
and yet when I consider the extent of his love,
the care he shows each day,
I really believe that he would;
that not only would he risk his life
but, if necessary, he'd give it, freely and gladly;
willing to die for us so that we might live!

Prayer

Loving God,
time and again we have gone astray from you.
You seek us out,
set us on our feet,
and we believe next time will be different,
but it's not:
once more we wander into error.
We are weak and foolish,
undeserving of your love,
yet still you reach out to us,
drawing us back to your side.

We praise you for the wonder of your grace,
for your willingness, through Christ,
to give your all for the sake of this world.
Lead us on through the changes and chances of this life,
and through the valley of the shadow of death,
until we are safely gathered into your kingdom
and the journey is done.
Amen.

10

What can I say, Lord?

David

Have mercy on me, O God, according to your steadfast love; according to your abundant mercy blot out my transgressions. Wash me thoroughly from my iniquity, and cleanse me from my sin. For I know my transgressions, and my sin is ever before me. Hide your face from my sins, and blot out all my iniquities. Create in me a clean heart, O God, and put a new and right spirit within me. Do not cast me away from your presence, and do not take your holy spirit from me. Restore to me the joy of your salvation, and sustain in me a willing heart.

Psalm 51:1–3, 9–12

Meditation

What can I say, Lord?
What *can* I say?
I've failed you again, haven't I?
Despite all my promises,
all my good intentions,
I've gone and let you down
like so many times before.
And I'm sickened,
crushed,
disgusted with myself,
ashamed I could be so pathetically weak,
so hopelessly false.
I tried so hard, that's what gets me down.
I was determined to make up for the lapses of the past,
to show you that I'm really serious about this business of discipleship,
and to prove that the trust you've shown in me,
your willingness to forgive and go on forgiving,
actually means something to me,
despite the way it may seem.
But could I do it?
No.

For a few hours, a few days, perhaps,
but finally I fell, as I always do, back into the old familiar ways.
Why, Lord?
What's wrong with me?
What am I going to do?
I can't change, not by myself.
I've tried it, and it's just no good,
the weaknesses running too deep,
too much a part of me for me to conquer them alone.
It's in your hands, Lord,
only *you* have the power to help me.
I know I don't deserve it,
that I've no claim on your love or mercy,
but I'm begging you,
pleading on bended knee,
pardon my iniquities.
Deal kindly, despite my folly;
cleanse my heart and renew my spirit.
Mould me,
fashion me,
forgive me,
restore me,
so that perhaps one day, by your grace,
I may serve as I should.
Lord, in your mercy, hear my prayer.

Prayer

Loving God,
it is easy to go through the motions of confession;
to claim we are sorry for our sin
and to make promises about our desire to serve you
without really thinking about what we are saying.
Familiarity leads us to take your grace for granted,
and so we fail to appreciate the gravity of letting you down.
Yet though your nature is always to have mercy,
you are grieved by our failings,
not least because they deny us fullness of life.
Help us, then, to see ourselves as we really are,
the bad as well as the good,
and give us genuine repentance,

so that we may receive the forgiveness you long to give,
and experience your transforming, renewing power,
through the grace of our Lord Jesus Christ.
Amen.

11

Could it be true?

Isaiah

In the year that King Uzziah died, I saw the Lord sitting on a throne, high and lofty; and the hem of his robe filled the temple. Seraphs were in attendance above him. And one called to another and said: 'Holy, holy, holy is the Lord of hosts; the whole earth is full of his glory.' And I said: 'Woe is me! I am lost, for I am a man of unclean lips, and I live among a people of unclean lips; yet my eyes have seen the King, the Lord of hosts!' Then one of the seraphs flew to me, holding a live coal that had been taken from the altar with a pair of tongs. The seraph touched my mouth with it and said: 'Now that this has touched your lips, your guilt has departed and your sin is blotted out.' Then I heard the voice of the Lord saying, 'Whom shall I send, and who will go for us?' And I said, 'Here am I; send me!'

Isaiah 6:1, 2a, 3, 5–8

Meditation

Could it be true?
Could God, in his mercy, forgive even me?
It seemed incredible,
too implausible for words,
for there was so much in my life not as it should be,
so many ways I daily let him down.
Does that surprise you,
me being a prophet and all that?
It shouldn't do,
for I was under no illusions as to my own importance,
not for a moment.
If God ever wanted to use me
it would be despite who I was, not because of it,
that's what I'd always imagined.
My faults were all too apparent to me,
and painful to contemplate.
I wanted to be different, don't get me wrong –
there was nothing I'd have liked better
than to offer faithful, unblemished service –

but there was no escaping reality:
I was as weak as the next man,
unable to resist temptation,
quick to go astray.
What reason was there to think I could change?
So when God appeared to me that day in the Temple,
I hate to say it, but I panicked,
consumed by a sense of my own unworthiness.
It was only a vision, I know,
but it brought home the shocking contrast
between his purity and my faults,
his strength and my weakness.
How could I ever bridge that gap?
There was no way I could even begin to.
Yet, next thing I knew, God reached out and touched me,
summoning me to service,
taking away my guilt,
making me whole.
Me, Isaiah, a prophet?
Could it be true?
Could God really make me new?
It seemed beyond belief,
childish, romantic nonsense!
Yet that's what he promised,
and that's what he's proved,
not just to me but to countless others across the years.
He called me to proclaim forgiveness,
a new start for all,
freedom from our sins.
And I've discovered, beyond all doubt,
the wonderful, astonishing truth of that message –
the simple, stupendous fact that whoever you are,
whatever you've done,
God is always ready to forgive what *has* been,
shape what *is*,
and transform what's yet to be.

Prayer

Gracious God,
we have no claim on your goodness,
no reason ever to expect mercy.
Despite our best intentions, time and again we fail you,
preferring our way to yours.
We say one thing, yet do another;
we claim to love you, yet openly flout your will.
Forgive us, for, try as we might, we cannot seem to help ourselves.
Renew us through your Spirit,
redeem us through your grace,
and remake us through your love
so that we may live and work for you,
to the glory of your name.
Amen.

12

I knew it would happen

Jonah

And the people of Nineveh believed God; they proclaimed a fast, and everyone, great and small, put on sackcloth. When God saw what they did, how they turned from their evil ways, God changed his mind about the calamity that he had said he would bring upon them; and he did not do it. But this was very displeasing to Jonah, and he became angry. He prayed to the Lord and said, ' O Lord! Is this not what I said while I was still in my own country? That is why I fled to Tarshish at the beginning; for I knew that you are a gracious God and merciful, slow to anger, and abounding in steadfast love, and ready to relent from punishing. And now, O Lord, please take my life from me, for it is better for me to die than to live.' And the Lord said, 'Is it right for you to be angry? Should I not be concerned about Nineveh, that great city, in which there are more than a hundred and twenty thousand persons who do not know their right hand from their left, and also many animals?'

Jonah 3:5, 10–4:4, 11

Meditation

I knew it would happen.
I just knew those wretched Ninevites would repent, given half a chance.
And that's precisely what they've done –
covered themselves in sackcloth and ashes,
grovelled in abject submission,
and begged him for mercy.
Can't he see through them?
Apparently not.
He's only too ready, it seems, to let bygones be bygones
and embrace them with open arms.
Isn't that just typical of him,
always ready to turn a blind eye the moment anyone claims to be sorry?
It's nauseating!
Honestly, can you blame me for running away like that
the moment he called me?
I knew immediately what his game was –

I've seen it happen all too often:
this God of ours is too soft by half.
Why waste time pussy-footing around, that's what I'd like to know?
There were no excuses for Nineveh.
They must have known all along that what they were doing was wrong,
the very name of the place being synonymous with corruption,
so why not just have done with it
and wipe them off the face of the earth,
put an end to them once and for all?
That's what I'd have done, and taken pleasure in it,
but not God, oh no.
He has to send muggins, here, doesn't he, to give them a warning,
knowing full well that, the moment they hear it,
they'll be fawning over him like lovesick fools.
It's his right, I accept that.
If he reckons they're worth saving
then that's his business and no else's.
But why did he have to choose *me*? –
that's what I find hard to stomach.
He knows my feelings on the matter,
what I'd do to those Ninevites given half the chance,
so surely he could have chosen someone more suited to the task.
I can't understand him, I really can't;
you'd almost think he wants to teach *me* a lesson as much as them.
Gracious, what am I saying?
Whatever next!

Prayer

Lord,
it's easy to talk about loving others;
much harder to mean it.
It's one thing to talk about forgiveness;
quite another to put it into practice.
There are some people we find hard to love and impossible to forgive.
We want them to suffer for the wrongs they've done,
pay the price for their actions,
and the thought of them getting off scot-free is hard to accept.
Yet if you dealt with us according to our deserving,
none of us could hope to escape punishment,
for we have all failed you in ways too many to number.

Help us to recognise that your grace
is greater than we can ever begin to imagine,
and may we rejoice in the wonder of your love that embraces all.
Amen.

13

Here's a funny thing

The woman at the well

Jesus answered her, 'If you knew the gift of God, and who it is that is saying to you, "Give me a drink," you would have asked him, and he would have given you living water.'

John 4:10

Meditation

Here's a funny thing:
one moment that Jesus fellow was asking me for water,
and the next he was promising the water of life,
bubbling up within,
a spring that never runs dry,
meeting my deepest need.
Very odd.
I should never have taken him on,
asking who he thought he was –
a Jew talking to a Samaritan like that,
a *man* approaching a woman on her own –
for suddenly it was *me* placed on the spot
and *him* asking the questions;
me apparently who was thirsty,
and *he* who could meet my need.
I was confused yet drawn in,
his words at once fascinating yet a puzzle,
for they revealed things above and secrets below,
holding out promise but also challenge.
He grasped better than I my inner longings
and knew my every fault,
yet, despite them all,
he seemed ready to grant me the blessings of which he spoke.
I still can't work it out,
for he made the first move,
apparently wanting something from me, if only a cup of water,

yet I left feeling that whatever I might give him
he can offer *me* far more.

Prayer

Lord Jesus Christ,
thank you for your love –
the joy, hope and peace you daily give,
the strength, mercy and blessing you unfailingly provide.
But, most of all,
thank you for asking nothing in return except that we receive;
that we open our hearts to you in glad and grateful response
and accept what you long to shower upon us.
Help us to celebrate the generosity of your grace,
the fullness of life you so freely offer.
Amen.

14

He had time for me

Matthew

As Jesus was walking along, he saw a man called Matthew sitting at the tax booth; and he said to him, 'Follow me.' And he got up and followed him. And as he sat at dinner in the house, many tax-collectors and sinners came and were sitting with him and his disciples. When the Pharisees saw this, they said to his disciples, 'Why does your teacher eat with tax-collectors and sinners?' But when he heard this, he said, 'Those who are well have no need of a physician, but those who are sick. Go and learn what this means, "I desire mercy, not sacrifice." For I have come to call not the righteous but sinners.'

Matthew 9:9–13

Meditation

He had time for me,
incredible, I know, but true.
He saw beneath the surface,
beneath the greed, selfishness and corruption,
and uncovered a person I didn't even know existed.
I groaned when I saw him coming, I won't pretend otherwise;
another self-righteous prig coming to tell me my business,
that's what I imagined.
And I'd had my fair share of those –
well, nobody likes a tax-collector, do they?
But I'd always given as good as I got.
I mean, it's not easy when you've a wife and kids at home to feed –
we all have to earn a living somehow –
and since the only people ready to give me a chance were the Romans,
what could I do?
Or did any of them really imagine I enjoyed working for them?
Anyway, someone had to do it, so why not me?
I suppose Jesus understood that, for he didn't criticise or condemn –
none of the two-faced hypocrisy of the Pharisees,
or the usual accusing glances and obscene gestures –

just those two lovely words: 'Follow me.'
You could have knocked me over.
It was the last thing I expected,
took the wind right out of my sails.
But more than that I was excited,
moved,
fascinated,
because he had time for me.
He hadn't written me off,
seen only the outside –
he accepted me as I was,
with all my sin sticking to me.
And the funny thing is, once he did that
it was me who pointed to my faults,
not him.
I felt ashamed,
painfully aware of all that was wrong,
longing to be different;
yet at the same time set free,
forgiven,
offered a new beginning.
I followed, of course,
What else could I do?
Would you refuse a man like that?
Well, perhaps you would, but I'm glad I didn't,
because despite everything since –
the times I've let him down,
the occasions I've misunderstood,
the mistakes I've made,
the faults I still have –
he goes on accepting me day after day,
not for what I might become,
but for what I am!

Prayer

Lord Jesus Christ,
we thank you that you love and accept us
not for what we can be but for what we are;
that although you see our many weaknesses,
still you have time for us,

seeing the best rather than the worst.
Forgive us that all too often we see only the surface,
judging people according to instant impressions,
and condemning those who do not fit in with our view of the world.
Help us to have time for others as you have time for us.
Amen.

15

I had a fig tree once

A landowner listening to Jesus

Then he told this parable: 'A man had a fig tree planted in his vineyard; and he came looking for fruit on it and found none. So he said to the gardener, "See here! For three years I have come looking for fruit on this fig tree, and still I find none. Cut it down! Why should it be wasting the soil?" He replied, "Sir, let it alone for one more year, until I dig round it and put manure on it. If it bears fruit next year, well and good; but if not, you can cut it down."'

Luke 13:6–9

Meditation

I had a fig tree once,
and, guess what:
I got rid of it.
It was just like the one in his parable,
barren,
not a hint of fruit,
so I got the gardener to cut it down
and plant another in its place.
Should I have waited perhaps?
Given it a little more time?
Maybe,
but I reckon, if I had, I'd still be twiddling my thumbs,
waiting in vain for that first crop.
We want results, don't we,
something to show for our efforts?
And when that fails to come, patience soon wears thin –
before long, exhausted.
Not so with Jesus.
Though we fail him time and again,
he perseveres with us,
refusing to write us off.
Though we promise much, yet yield nothing,

repeatedly he forgives,
always ready to offer another chance.
Is your faith as fruitful as it should be?
Mine isn't,
nowhere near –
it's barely fruitful *at all*.
Yet those words of Jesus give me heart,
for though *I* give up believing I can ever change,
he does not.

Prayer

Gracious Lord,
we despair of ourselves sometimes,
for we repeatedly fail you,
foolishly, stubbornly and rebelliously flouting your will.
Thank you for not giving up on us
though we feel like doing so ourselves,
for patiently and lovingly forgiving our faults
and offering us chance after chance to start again.
Help us to grow in faith, love and commitment,
so that we might finally bear fruit for you.
Amen.

16

They brought home to me, those words of his in Jerusalem

Mary Magdalene

'Jerusalem, Jerusalem, the city that kills the prophets and stones those who are sent to it! How often have I desired to gather your children together as a hen gathers her brood under her wings, and you were not willing!'

Luke 13:34

Meditation

They brought home to me, those words of his in Jerusalem,
just how much he cared,
for there was real sorrow in his voice,
real pain,
real anguish.
He wasn't just playing a part,
going through the motions,
as though his time on earth were some necessary evil
before he could return to heaven.
He was committed to us,
passionately concerned,
his heart aching for all to know his love,
taste his blessing,
experience his joy.
But though he longed to embrace us,
as a mother cradles her child,
a hen gathers her brood,
he didn't compel anyone to accept,
respecting rather their right to refuse.
And, tragically, many did just that,
his message and purpose passing them by.
He continued regardless,
resolute to the end,
not even hatred and rejection deflecting his love,

but though he gave his all to redeem his own,
still they would not hear.
He's risen now,
triumphant over death and exalted on high,
but don't think that means he's detached,
remote,
indifferent to our needs.
He still cares as passionately as ever –
for you,
for me,
for everyone –
more than we will ever know.
Respond . . .
and receive.

Prayer

Saviour Christ,
thank you that we matter to you,
that you truly care about our welfare.
Thank you that, whatever we do,
you never stop loving us;
that however often we push you away,
you reach out still,
longing to welcome us into your embrace.
Help us to understand the depth of your devotion,
and to receive the blessing you so long to give.
Amen.

17

Not much of a story, is it?

Simon the Pharisee

'A certain creditor had two debtors; one owed five hundred denarii, and the other fifty. When they could not pay, he cancelled the debts for both of them. Now which of them will love him more?'

Luke 7:41, 42

Meditation

Not much of a story, is it?
In fact, you can hardly call it that, can you?
More of a throwaway line really –
or so at least you might have thought had you not been there.
But the thing is, I *was*!
I was sitting right there in the house of Simon,
feasting with his family and friends,
and I'd watched open-mouthed with the rest of them
as that woman strolled in,
kneeling down to bathe the feet of Jesus with her tears.
What an exhibition!
We were disgusted,
for we all knew the kind of person she was,
and we were appalled that anyone could be so forward,
so brazen,
as to barge in like that,
let alone presume her attentions were welcomed.
It was only a matter of time before someone said
what we were all thinking,
and it was Simon who eventually broke the silence,
muttering low under his breath.
'How could Jesus just sit there smiling?' he wanted to know.
'How could he even be near such a woman,
let alone allow her to touch him?
What sort of man was he?
Not a prophet, clearly!'

And that's when Jesus turned to us and told that story.
How did it go down?
Let me put it this way: a storm was brewing,
for we all knew what he was suggesting
even before he spelt it out for us.
He actually believed that God had time for this woman,
that, despite all she'd done,
her sordid, seedy past,
she could still find forgiveness and a place in his kingdom.
Amazing!
Yet if that wasn't shocking enough, there was worse,
for, according to him,
she wasn't the only one who'd had her debts cancelled;
it was *us* too,
or at least it could be if only we were ready to admit our need!
Can you believe it!
He was claiming the power to forgive sins,
even seeming to suggest that our response to *him*
determines *God's* response to *us*.
We could have stoned him for that, you know,
and very possibly would have,
but for one thing:
the look on that woman's face as she walked away,
an expression of such peace, joy and gratitude that I shall never forget it.
She was evidently at one with God,
her soul at rest,
and, though I hate to admit it,
I longed to share what she'd discovered.
Who knows, one day,
just maybe,
I may find the courage to confess my need
and respond in turn.

Prayer

Lord Jesus Christ,
you have been merciful to us in so much;
forgive us that we show mercy in so little.
You see what is best in us;
forgive us that we see what is worst in others.
You receive us as we are;

forgive us that *our* acceptance of people
depends on them becoming what we would have them be.
You have time for us all;
forgive us that we have time only for ourselves.
Though we deserve so little you love us so much;
help us to love you in return.
Work *in* us,
that we may work *for* you.
Amen.

18

Lost?

A listener to Jesus

He told them this parable: 'Which one of you, having a hundred sheep and losing one of them, does not leave the ninety-nine in the wilderness and go after the one that is lost until he finds it? When he has found it, he lays it on his shoulders and rejoices. And when he comes home, he calls together his friends and neighbours, saying to them, "Rejoice with me, for I have found my sheep that was lost." Just so, I tell you, there will be more joy in heaven over one sinner who repents than over ninety-nine righteous persons who need no repentance.'

Luke 15:3–7

Meditation

Lost?
You can say that again!
I hadn't just gone astray,
I'd gone over the edge,
plunged into the deepest pit,
and I was scrabbling in the mud,
sinking ever deeper into a mire of my own making,
no prospect of escape.
I wanted to get out, of course I did,
nothing I would have liked more than to make my peace with God
and start again.
But what hope was there for someone like me?
I dare not tell you the things I'd done –
mistakes too foolish, too shameful even to name,
a sorry catalogue of failure.
Could God forgive all that?
Surely not.
He'd wash his hands of me at best,
but, more likely, reach out to punish,
his anger burning against me,
his fury rightly kindled.

Isn't that the sort of God he is:
vengeful and jealous,
a God of justice and righteousness,
unable even to look upon evil?
That's what I'd always been told,
and that's why I'd resigned myself to my fate.
So you can imagine my surprise that day when Jesus came by
and, in the space of a few words, turned my world on its head.
He spoke of a God who not only forgives but comes looking for us,
seeking us out with infinite patience,
never resting until we are found;
a God who picks us up and carries us on his shoulders,
exulting in our return and gently restoring us to the fold.
I can't explain it, for I've never encountered love like that before,
never even knew it existed.
All I can say is this:
I was lost,
stumbling blindly in the darkness,
and, in my need, Jesus found me,
and brought me safely home!

Prayer

Lord Jesus Christ,
thank you for watching over us throughout our lives,
continually there to guard and guide, whatever we may face.
When we wander far from your side
you do not abandon us to our fate,
but instead come looking for us,
your love refusing to let us go.
Though we forsake you, you never forsake us.
Though we are faithless, you remain faithful.
Forgive us all the ways we continue to go astray,
and help us to follow you more closely in the days ahead.
Amen.

19

It's true what he said, isn't it?

A listener to Jesus

'Or what woman having ten silver coins, if she loses one of them, does not light a lamp, sweep the house, and search carefully until she finds it? When she has found it, she calls together her friends and neighbours, saying, "Rejoice with me, for I have found the coin that I had lost." Just so, I tell you, there is joy in the presence of the angels of God over one sinner who repents.'

Luke 15:8–10

Meditation

It's true what he said, isn't it?
You can just imagine that woman,
searching the house from top to bottom,
pulling back the furniture,
brushing away the cobwebs,
rummaging around in the nooks and crannies,
her frustration mounting all the while,
until at last, joy of joys, the coin is found!
I've done similar myself, many a time –
the picture all too familiar –
and, yes, when you finally come up trumps
you can get carried away,
your sense of satisfaction out of all proportion
to what it was you were looking for.
Why do we search so earnestly?
Because no matter how trivial the sum involved,
we know it's worth something,
and we don't like to see good money go to waste.
But can we really apply that to the way God feels about us?
I'd like to think so,
but I have my doubts,
for, much though I'd like to believe it,
are any of us worth that much,
enough for him to put himself out on our behalf,

spend time seeking us out,
and actually rejoice when he finds us?
I find that hard to swallow, I'm afraid,
for, when I look at my life,
the fact is I feel pretty worthless sometimes,
so little there of value,
so much that is cheap and empty.
It's not just the mistakes I make,
evil I do,
folly I'm guilty of,
though there's enough of that and more.
No, it's the good things, too:
my love,
my acts of kindness,
my rare attempts at service,
for even those are tainted,
more about myself than others,
my own kudos rather than their welfare.
Could God conceivably be bothered one way or another
about our ultimate fate,
whether we accept or reject him,
love or loathe him?
Would he even consider wasting time on people like us?
It's a staggering idea, isn't it,
understandably hard to accept,
but that's what Jesus is saying,
that each of us is not just worth something,
but special,
precious in God's sight,
important enough for him to go on looking for us,
day after day,
until his search is finally rewarded.
I didn't believe it,
and I'm not sure I do even now,
yet I'm beginning to wonder,
for, despite my doubts and questions,
my repeated rejection,
Jesus clearly hasn't given up on me,
or anyone else, as far as I can see,
our lives really seeming to matter to him.
Maybe, just maybe,
it could be true.

Prayer

Lord Jesus Christ,
it's wonderful enough that when we were lost you came and found us;
it's more wonderful still that you continue to seek us out
when we go astray again;
that you go on looking for us,
day after day,
year after year,
for as long as it takes,
as often as it is needed.
No matter who we are or what we may have done,
still we matter to you,
enough for you never to rest until we are restored to your side.
Teach us to recognise the astonishing breadth of your love,
and gratefully to respond.
Amen.

20

Lost and found!

An early Christian

'But while he was still far off, his father saw him and was filled with compassion; he ran and put his arms around him and kissed him. Then the son said to him, "Father, I have sinned against heaven and before you; I am no longer worthy to be called your son." But the father said to his slaves, "Quickly, bring out a robe – the best one – and put it on him; put a ring on his finger and sandals on his feet. And get the fatted calf and kill it, and let us eat and celebrate; for this son of mine was dead and is alive again; he was lost and is found!" And they began to celebrate.'

Luke 15:20b–24

Meditation

Lost and found!
It wasn't the first parable he'd told on that theme,
but to me it was the best;
those words of his, when I heard them,
falling like music on my ears,
for though the message was much the same as before,
the implications were so very different.
I was just like that young man, you see,
the second of the two sons,
not simply lost but having wilfully gone astray.
I'd known and understood the Father's love,
what it was to be part of his family,
and I'd gone and frittered it all away,
preferring my way to his,
squandering the riches he'd given me,
living with no thought of his will or guidance.
It was my own doing, no one else's.
I'd plumbed the depths of despair,
sunk until I could sink no lower,
and it was all down to me;
a self-made humiliation.
That's what frightened me the most:

to be lost is one thing –
anyone can make a mistake –
but to be the knowing instrument of your own destruction,
to recognise the error of your ways and carry on regardless,
can God forgive that?
I thought he'd washed his hands of me,
that if I dared approach him he'd shoo me away,
so I kept my distance and lived with my shame as best I could.
Only, suddenly, here was Jesus speaking not just of forgiveness
but of joyful acceptance,
a love reaching out to meet me,
celebrating my return,
welcoming me home,
and it dawned on me that the mercy of God
is far greater than I'd realised.
I'd walked away,
and assumed there could be no return.
But I was wrong,
for he was there waiting,
arms outstretched to receive me back.
I was lost,
and now I'm found!

Prayer

Lord Jesus Christ,
we find it hard enough to forgive mistakes made unintentionally against us,
but when they are deliberate, resentment and bitterness builds up within us.
Yet day after day we are guilty of just such disobedience to God,
ignoring his guidance,
flouting his will
and breaking his commandments.
We know we do wrong
and yet still we do it,
our faith weak and the power of temptation strong.
By our own standards we deserve no mercy,
yet you tell us that God is always waiting to welcome us back,
ready to forgive our failure and help us to start again.
Receive our grateful worship
and help us to live more faithfully as your people.
Amen.

21

Which would I have been most disappointed with?

A mother listening to the parable of the lost son

'Son, you are always with me, and all that is mine is yours. But we had to celebrate and rejoice, because this brother of yours was dead and has come to life; he was lost and has been found.'

Luke 15:31, 32

Meditation

Which would I have been most disappointed with:
the son who came back
or the one who stayed at home?
It's a tough call,
for they both had their fair share of faults,
the first wild and wanton,
the second shrivelled in spirit –
hardly a pair to write home about.
Initially, though, I sided with the 'dutiful' son,
for, after all, *he* didn't fritter away his inheritance,
demean himself through loose living:
a shocking senseless waste if ever there was one.
But give the younger son this:
he had the humility to admit his mistakes
and enough respect for his father
to believe he still might receive some welcome from him,
if only as a hired hand.
It takes some doing swallowing your pride,
admitting your faults and standing up to face the music.
The elder son, by contrast, may have *seemed* faithful,
but he clearly believed he was owed something,
his love and loyalty not unconditional but with strings attached,
expecting a reward for good behaviour.
It's just a story, of course, I recognise that,

but, as with all those Jesus told, it pays thinking about,
for it holds lessons we do well to learn.
If you think you've earned God's favour, you're sadly mistaken.
If you recognise you haven't, you're halfway to finding it.
That's the message:
though we deserve nothing, God delights to give.
Love him, then, for the joy of doing so,
not for anything you might receive.
Recognise your faults and receive forgiveness
instead of begrudging it to others.
In our own way every one of us fails him, time and again,
but as Jesus so wonderfully showed,
he never fails *us*.

Prayer

Thank you, Lord, for your free and total love,
poured out though it meets rejection in response,
enduring though it is betrayed,
extended again and again however often it is ignored.
Forgive us that, by contrast,
our love for *you* is flawed and partial,
blowing hot and cold, dependent on circumstances.
Teach us to respond to you with no thought of reward;
to give, not for what we can get,
but rather for what we can offer back to you
who offered so much for all.
Amen.

22

What would you have done, had it been you?

Peter

Then he told this parable: 'A man had a fig tree planted in his vineyard; and he came looking for fruit on it and found none. So he said to the gardener, "See here! For three years I have come looking for fruit on this fig tree, and still I find none. Cut it down! Why should it be wasting the soil?" He replied, "Sir, let it alone for one more year, until I dig around it and put manure on it. If it bears fruit next year, well and good; but if not, you can cut it down."'

Luke 13:6–9

Meditation

What would you have done, had it been you,
had you come to that fig tree you'd planted
and found, yet again, no sign of fruit on it,
nothing to justify the time and expense spent on its cultivation?
Would you have waited another year,
given it one more chance to blossom despite your disappointment,
or would you have abandoned it as a bad job,
ordered it to be dug up to make room for a better specimen,
one more likely to reward your investment?
Remember, this wasn't a first-year planting –
it should have been yielding a plentiful harvest long since,
and the likelihood is that no fruit one year means no fruit the next –
what reason to expect any change?
Only, of course, it wasn't finally a fig tree Jesus was talking about here –
it was people like you and me
and the harvest we produce in our lives,
or, at least, the harvest we're meant to produce.
Sadly, it's all too often a different story –
despite the care and attention God has lavished on us,
the patient preparation and dedicated nurture,
there's precious little to show for it,

no harvest worthy of the name.
Why bother with us any further?
What reason to expect any sentiment from God,
any chance to atone for past failures?
None at all.
And yet, like the gardener in the parable,
Jesus continually pleads our cause.
One more year, he begs,
one last opportunity for us to make amends –
justice tempered by mercy,
righteousness by grace.
So is the next chance our last one?
Is that what Jesus was saying to his listeners,
his words intended as a stern final warning?
You might have thought so, mightn't you? –
and, yes, I suppose the day may come
when God's patience will indeed be exhausted
and the axe has to fall.
Yet don't despair,
for, while we shouldn't take it for granted,
the wonderful thing is this:
year after year Jesus goes on asking we be given one more chance,
and year after year God continues to grant that request.

Prayer

Lord Jesus Christ,
we know the fruits you want to see in our lives:
love,
joy,
peace,
patience,
kindness,
generosity,
faithfulness,
gentleness
and self-control.
We know we ought to show these,
and we know also how rarely we do,
how the fruits we produce tend to be very different.
Instead of living by the Spirit we live by the flesh,

and the results are plain for all to see.
Forgive us,
and by your grace grant us another chance to start again.
Put your Spirit within us
and nurture our faith
so that the time will come when our lives will bear a rich harvest
to the glory of your name.
Amen.

23

So you've made a mistake, have you?

Peter

'The kingdom of heaven may be compared to a king who wished to settle accounts with his slaves. When he began the reckoning, one who owed him ten thousand talents was brought to him; and, as he could not pay, his lord ordered him to be sold, together with his wife and children and all his possessions, and payment to be made. So the slave fell on his knees before him, saying, "Have patience with me, and I will pay you everything." And out of pity for him, the lord of that slave released him and forgave him the debt. But that same slave, as he went out, came upon one of his fellow slaves who owed him a hundred denarii; and seizing him by the throat, he said, "Pay what you owe." Then his fellow slave fell down and pleaded with him, "Have patience with me, and I will pay you." But he refused; then he went and threw him into prison until he would pay the debt. When his fellow slaves saw what had happened, they were greatly distressed, and they went and reported to their lord all that had taken place. Then his lord summoned him and said to him, "You wicked slave! I forgave you all that debt because you pleaded with me. Should you not have had mercy on your fellow slave, as I had mercy on you?" And in anger his lord handed him over to be tortured until he would pay his entire debt. So my heavenly Father will also do to every one of you, if you do not forgive your brother or sister from your heart.'

Matthew 18:23–35

Meditation

So you've made a mistake, have you?
Done something foolish?
Don't worry, God will forgive you.
You've spoken rashly,
caused offence?
Never mind, God will understand.
You've acted selfishly,
ignored the needy?
No matter, God is gracious.
Is that how you tend to think?

I did!
I had this picture of God as all-forgiving,
all-merciful,
'slow to anger and abounding in steadfast love' –
you know the kind of thing:
in short, a soft touch,
though I'd never have put it so crudely.
Oh yes, I was well aware of what Jesus had told us,
those words of his concerning prayer –
'Forgive us our sins, as *we* forgive those who sin against *us*' –
but I never imagined he meant us to take that literally,
never for a moment really thought he was serious.
Only, as I sat and listened to that parable, a cold chill came over me,
for I realised he meant every word.
The grace of God,
his goodness and mercy –
it's not just doled out willy-nilly,
extended indiscriminately, come what may.
It's a free gift, true,
one we can never earn, however hard we try,
but if, having received mercy, we fail to show it to others,
then what God has given he can just as easily take away.
He sets no price on his forgiveness,
but he expects a response,
an expression of gratitude not just in words but deeds,
and, ultimately, the measure we give is the measure we'll get.
You find that disturbing?
You're not the only one,
for it shatters our cosy, comfortable illusions,
but I tell you this:
better to shatter such a picture now,
while there's still time to put things right,
than one day to find it broken for us,
and discover it's too late to make amends!

Prayer

Lord Jesus Christ,
through your suffering and death
you paid the price that we could never begin to pay.
You gave your all so that the debt we owe might be cancelled,
our freedom secured through your offering of love.
Yet, having been forgiven so much,
we are willing to forgive so little.
We dwell on mistakes made against us,
we nurse grievances,
we look for revenge,
we are swift to judge and eager to condemn.
Have mercy on us yet again,
and put a right spirit within us.
Teach us to remember all you have done for us,
and so may we reach out to others,
ready to show mercy in turn –
to forgive,
to forget,
to love
and to accept.
Amen.

24

Which am I, I wondered?

A rabbi listening to Jesus

He also told this parable to some who trusted in themselves that they were righteous and regarded others with contempt. 'Two men went up to the temple to pray, one a Pharisee and the other a tax-collector. The Pharisee, standing by himself, was praying thus, "God, I thank you that I am not like other people: thieves, rogues, adulterers, or even like this tax-collector. I fast twice a week; I give a tenth of all my income." But the tax-collector, standing far off, would not even look up to heaven, but was beating his breast and saying, "God, be merciful to me, a sinner!" I tell you, this man went home justified rather than the other; for all who exalt themselves will be humbled, but all who humble themselves will be exalted.'

Luke 18:9–14

Meditation

Which am I, I wondered:
the Pharisee, or the tax-collector?
I'm neither, of course,
not literally,
but that wasn't the point was it?
'Which of the two do I most resemble?'
that's what I found myself asking,
and I had a shrewd suspicion I wouldn't much like the answer.
So it proved,
though perhaps not quite as I feared,
for, in actual fact – like most of us, I suspect – I'm a bit of both,
neither all of one nor all of the other.
There are times when I'm the tax-collector –
overwhelmed by a sense of failure,
able only to throw myself on God's goodness,
knowing I have no claim on his love
nor any reason to expect mercy.
And at those times, just as Jesus said, I find a sense of peace,
a feeling of being put right with God –

my sins forgiven,
the past absolved,
mistakes over and done with.
Only it never lasts,
for there's always that other self refusing to be silenced,
the Pharisee within me straining to break free –
prim, proper, self-righteous,
head shaking in disapproval,
finger pointing in accusation,
so certain I am right and others are wrong.
Can they both be me,
each part of the same person?
I'm afraid they are, much though it hurts to admit it.
But at least it *does* hurt, that's something,
for so long as I can still see the truth,
still see myself as I really am,
and still feel a sense of shame,
then all is not lost –
there's hope for me even yet.
So I'm here, Lord,
the two of me together,
tax-collector and Pharisee,
and my prayer is simply this:
'God, be merciful to me, a sinner!'

Prayer

Lord Jesus Christ,
we do not mean to be self-righteous,
but we are,
more often than we may realise.
We claim to be accepting of others,
but when they do not conform to our expectations
we make little attempt to conceal our feelings.
We claim to recognise our faults,
but if anyone points them out to us
we are quick to take offence.
We see the speck in our neighbour's eye
but time and again overlook the log in our own.
Forgive us our innate tendency to assume that we are right
and others are wrong.

Help us, instead, to understand that, whoever we are,
we depend finally on your grace,
and so, recognising the strengths and weaknesses of all,
may we live in true humility
to the glory of your name.
Amen.

25

Do you remember that parable Jesus told?

Andrew

'For the kingdom of heaven is like a landowner who went out early in the morning to hire labourers for his vineyard. After agreeing with the labourers for the usual daily wage, he sent them into his vineyard. When he went out about nine o'clock, he saw others standing idle in the marketplace; and he said to them, "You also go into the vineyard, and I will pay you whatever is right." So they went. When he went out again about noon and about three o'clock, he did the same. And about five o'clock he went out and found others standing around; and he said to them, "Why are you standing here idle all day?" They said to him, "Because no one has hired us." He said to them, "You also go into the vineyard." When evening came, the owner of the vineyard said to his manager, "Call the labourers and give them their pay, beginning with the last and then going to the first." When those hired about five o'clock came, each of them received the usual daily wage. Now when the first came, they thought they would receive more; but each of them also received the usual daily wage. And when they received it, they grumbled against the landowner, saying, "These last worked only one hour, and you have made them equal to us who have borne the burden of the day and the scorching heat." But he replied to one of them, "Friend, I am doing you no wrong; did you not agree with me for the usual daily wage? Take what belongs to you and go; I choose to give to this last the same as I give to you. Am I not allowed to do what I choose with what belongs to me? Or are you envious because I am generous?" So the last will be first, and the first will be last.'

Matthew 20:1–16

Meditation

Do you remember that parable Jesus told –
the one about the father and the two sons,
the eldest of whom complained bitterly
when his brother was welcomed back
with open arms after having wantonly frittered away his inheritance?
Well, it seems to me that, in his story of the vineyard,

he's provided a sort of sequel,
for it's on much the same theme:
the apparently indiscriminate nature of God's grace.
It's hard, isn't it, not to feel a certain sympathy for that older brother,
hardhearted though he may have been?
But, compared to those labourers in the vineyards –
the ones taken on first thing in the morning –
there's no comparison,
the sense of injustice their treatment evokes
being almost impossible to overcome.
How would you have felt had you been toiling away there all day,
sweating under the noonday sun,
only to see a succession of late recruits swan along at the last minute
and walk away with the same payment for their efforts as you?
Hardly fair, is it?
In fact, it's precisely the sort of thing
that would have even the mildest of folk up in arms,
storming off to the boss to protest about their rights.
Only what's fair in God's book is not the same as in ours,
his thoughts not being our thoughts,
nor his ways our ways.
He calls *whom* he wishes, *when* he wishes,
granting his blessing *where* he sees fit, *as* he sees fit.
and ours is not to reason why.
Don't forget, none of us deserve his love;
it's *his gift* rather than *our right*.
And don't forget also that, when it comes to serving God,
the reward is in the doing as much as in the ultimate prize,
those who come to faith late
having missed out on a lifetime of fulfilment
rather than having filched unwarranted riches.
Remember that next time God calls someone you deem undeserving
and you're inclined to raise an eyebrow at his mercy.
Stop, and think again,
or you may find that,
far from receiving only the same reward as them,
you receive no reward at all!

Prayer

Lord Jesus Christ,
we know that your kingdom is not of this world
and yet still sometimes we can't help judging by this world's standards.
We have a fixed idea in our minds of those you find acceptable,
those worthy or unworthy to receive your love;
and we regard some as better Christians than others,
more deserving of your goodness,
more entitled to your blessing,
the service they offer and faith they show surely meriting special favour.
Yet that merely betrays our misunderstanding of your love –
your sovereign grace that gives freely to *all* though *none* deserve it,
that offers a new quality of life simply through the joy of knowing you.
Teach us never to measure people by our flawed human values
but to recognise that everyone, whoever they are, matters to you,
and may that be all we need to know.
Amen.

26

He made it all sound so easy

The scribe

One of the scribes came near and heard them disputing with one another, and seeing that Jesus answered them well, he asked him, 'Which commandment is the first of all?' Jesus answered, 'The first is, "Hear, O Israel: the Lord our God, the Lord is one; you shall love the Lord your God with all your heart, and with all your soul, and with all your mind, and with all your strength." The second is this, "You shall love your neighbour as yourself." There is no other commandment greater than these.'

Mark 12:28–31

Meditation

He made it all sound so easy,
so simple.
The whole Law,
everything we'd been struggling to understand for so many years,
summed up in two little commandments:
you shall love the Lord your God with all your heart and mind and soul;
you shall love your neighbour as yourself.
It sounds perfect, doesn't it?
What our faith is all about, in a nutshell.
And for the most part I agreed with him –
spot on!
Love God, love your neighbour;
I've no problem with that –
it's what I've tried to do all my life.
But love your neighbour as yourself –
that's where I come unstuck;
for though you may not believe it,
and though it may rarely seem like it,
I don't love myself at all.
Oh, I give a good impression, I know.
I'm as selfish as the next person,

invariably putting *my* interests before those of others,
more often than not wrapped up in my own affairs –
I can't deny that.
But beneath the facade,
whenever I have the courage to look deep inside,
I'm ashamed of what I see,
ashamed of what I am.
Love myself?
With all my weakness, greed, pride?
You must be joking!
Only he wasn't, that's the mystery;
there was no irony from Jesus when he said those words,
no sarcasm or hidden agenda.
Love your neighbour as yourself, he told us,
and he meant it;
he actually believed that I was lovable.
I just can't tell you what that means,
what hope it gives me –
him to say such a thing of all people!
For he was under no illusions,
no false sense of my worthiness.
He knew me as I was, better than anyone,
with all my faults and ugliness,
yet he still believed I was worth something.
Am I convinced?
Well, not as much as I'd like to be,
for there are still times when I look at myself and turn away in shame.
I'm not pretty,
not special,
not a nice person at all when you get down to it.
But I've begun to understand that inside this stranger I call me,
beneath the mask I put on for the world,
there's a person who God truly values,
an individual unique and precious to him,
and if *he* believes that, despite everything,
who am *I* to argue?

Prayer

Gracious God,
we marvel that you can love us,
for there is so little about us that deserves it.
We look into the mirror of our souls
and are repelled by what we see there,
for the image is marred by so much.
Yet, incredibly, you value us
to the point that we are precious in your sight,
special enough even to die for.
If *you* can accept us despite everything,
teach us to do the same,
and, in learning to love ourselves as you do,
help us also to love others and you.
Amen.

27

I expected him to condemn me, like all the rest

The woman caught in adultery

The scribes and the Pharisees brought a woman who had been caught in adultery; and making her stand before all of them, they said to him, 'Teacher, this woman was caught in the very act of committing adultery. Now in the law Moses commanded us to stone such women. Now what do you say?' They said this to test him, so that they might have some charge to bring against him. Jesus bent down and wrote with his finger on the ground. When they kept on questioning him, he straightened up and said to them, 'Let anyone among you who is without sin be the first to throw a stone at her.' And once again he bent down and wrote on the ground. When they heard it, they went away, one by one, beginning with the elders; and Jesus was left alone with the woman standing before him. Jesus straightened up and said to her, 'Woman, where are they? Has no one condemned you?' She said, 'No one, sir.' And Jesus said, 'Neither do I condemn you. Go your way, and from now on do not sin again.'

John 8:3–11

Meditation

I expected him to condemn me, like all the rest,
to shake his head in disgust and send me to my death.
Just another self-righteous busybody, that's what I thought –
you know the sort,
the kind always up on their soap-box,
sounding off about something or other,
telling folk how they ought to live their lives.
Not that it mattered much this time who he was,
for there was no getting away from it:
I'd broken the Law,
caught, as they say, well and truly in the act –
no way anyone could get me out of that one,
even if they'd wished to.
And you could see from the smug look of the Pharisees

that they felt the same –
lips twisted with contempt,
eyes glittering with hatred,
their hands positively itching to pick up the first stone
and strike me down.
It was just a matter of time,
a question of completing the necessary formalities
before the verdict was given.
So I cowered there trembling,
waiting for the fateful signal for them to begin,
expecting each moment to be my last.
I waited . . .
and I waited . . .
sweat trickling down my brow,
limbs shaking in terror . . .
But it didn't happen,
no word,
no sign,
nothing.
What could it mean?
A reprieve?
Surely not.
But what then?
Some heartless trick to prolong my agony,
an unforeseen last-minute technicality,
or simply a pause while they gathered the rocks to stone me?
There was only one way to find out,
so I looked up,
tense,
fearful . . .
then stopped,
transfixed,
catching my breath in astonishment,
for we were alone,
just the two of us,
me and Jesus,
not another soul to be seen.
I thought I was dreaming for a moment,
either that or the stoning had despatched me unbeknown to another life.
But then he spoke,
his eyes gentle yet piercing as he voiced my unspoken question:

'Woman, where are your accusers?'
They were gone, each one of them,
none able, apparently, to throw the first stone;
and even as I struggled to take it in, he spoke again,
those marvellous, memorable words:
'Neither do I condemn you.'
I should have danced for joy, shouldn't I? –
whooped with delight,
laughed in exultation –
for I was free,
not simply reprieved but forgiven,
invited to go back and start again.
But I didn't laugh.
I broke down in tears,
the sobs convulsing my body,
tears streaming down my face,
for suddenly, faced by this astonishing man,
I saw myself as I really was . . .
and became my own accuser.
I'd expected death, and been given life,
feared judgement, and been shown mercy;
what had seemed the end was suddenly a new beginning –
and it was all too much to take in!
Not any more, though.
I understand now what he's done for me,
and I look back to that day with wonder,
my whole being throbbing with praise,
for he met me in my need and made me whole,
saw me at my worst,
and dared to believe the best!

Prayer

Lord Jesus Christ,
you did not come to judge or condemn the world,
but in order to save it.
Where others saw the bad in people,
you saw the good.
You recognised the value in everyone,
and instilled in them a sense of worth,
scandalising many by your willingness to accept the unacceptable.

Forgive our tendency to be self-righteous,
more concerned with judgement than mercy.
Forgive our failure to see in ourselves
the evil we so readily see in others.
Teach us to look at the world with your eyes,
and to deal graciously in all our relationships,
just as you have dealt graciously with us.
Amen.

28

Was it even a prayer, that cry of the tax-collector?

A listener to the parable of the Pharisee and the tax-collector

'But the tax-collector, standing far off, would not even look up to heaven, but was beating his breast and saying, "God, be merciful to me, a sinner!" I tell you, this man went down to his home justified rather than the other.'

Luke 18:13, 14a

Meditation

Was it even a prayer, that cry of the tax-collector?
Think about it:
he refused to approach God,
wouldn't even look towards heaven
so great was his sense of unworthiness –
his utter guilt and shame.
Don't ask me what he'd done,
but it was clearly nothing to be proud about,
and the fellow knew it.
The Pharisee, by contrast, may have been a touch self-righteous,
smug even,
but give him his due,
he'd have observed the Law to the letter,
scrupulous in every detail.
Can you really ask for more than that?
Tell me, which of the two would you have kept company with,
given the choice?
Which would you have trusted with your money,
your children,
your life?
Do I need to ask?
No, the Pharisees have their faults, certainly,
but they're devout,
upright,

God-fearing –
decent and respectable folk like you and me.
So what was Jesus thinking of telling a story like that?
Honestly, he'll give religion a bad name with such talk,
as if all our dutiful devotion can somehow be worth less
than a single cry from the heart.
Surely not even *he* can mean that!
Can he?

Prayer

Lord Jesus Christ, forgive us,
for we fail you time and again,
betraying and denying your love.
We are weak, stubborn, proud, foolish,
false and faithless in so much.
Cleanse us from our faults
for they are ever before us.
Have mercy, Lord,
have mercy.
Amen.

29

It took me a long time to grasp it

John the Evangelist

'For God so loved the world that he gave his only Son, so that everyone who believes in him may not perish but may have eternal life.'

John 3:16

Meditation

It took me a long time to grasp it,
a lifetime of reflection on what his life,
death and resurrection actually mean,
but finally the truth crystallised in a few simple words:
'God so loved the world that he gave his only Son'.
It's simple, isn't it?
Yet somehow, with the best of intentions,
we make it instead so complex.
To hear some people talk,
believers included,
you'd think God feels just the opposite:
that he's concerned to judge rather than bless,
condemn rather than forgive,
punish rather than redeem.
'Believe this' they say,
'believe that',
commitment becoming a matter of jumping through the right hoops,
and woe betide us if we don't.
But that's *their* message,
not his;
a reflection of how much we struggle to accept his sheer grace,
his wholly undeserved love and pardon.
He asks merely that we *believe* in him –
no more,
no less.
Do that, and we will discover the secret of eternal life,

and, ridiculous though it may seem,
contradicting our every sense of justice and fair play,
we will receive that gift not because *we* love *God*
but because *he* loves *us*.

Prayer

Sovereign God,
the words trip off the tongue easily enough:
that yours is the way of love,
that you loved the world enough to die for it,
that you are love itself –
but though we accept such ideas in theory,
in practice we struggle to accept the wonder of their message,
setting instead human limits to your grace and goodness.
Our own love is partial, flawed, conditional,
as much about ourselves as others,
and we subconsciously expect yours to be the same,
somehow dependent on us doing, saying or being the right thing.
Open our hearts to your gracious mercy that accepts us as we are –
to your love that will never let us go.
Amen.

30

Have you ever tried turning over a new leaf?

The Apostle Paul

For we know that the law is spiritual; but I am of the flesh, sold into slavery under sin. I do not understand my own actions. For I do not do what I want, but I do the very thing I hate. Now if I do what I do not want, I agree that the law is good. But in fact it is no longer I that do it, but sin that dwells within me. For I know that nothing good dwells within me, that is, in my flesh. I can will what is right, but I cannot do it. For I do not do the good I want, but the evil I do not want is what I do. Now if I do what I do not want, it is no longer I that do it, but sin that dwells within me. So I find it to be a law that when I want to do what is good, evil lies close at hand. For I delight in the law of God in my inmost self, but I see in my members another law at war with the law of my mind, making me captive to the law of sin that dwells in my members. Wretched man that I am! Who will rescue me from this body of death? Thanks be to God through Jesus Christ our Lord! So then, with my mind I am a slave to the law of God, but with my flesh I am a slave to the law of sin.

Romans 7:14–25

Meditation

Have you ever tried turning over a new leaf?
I have,
again . . .
and again . . .
and again.
Every morning I wake up and say,
'Today is going to be different!'
And every night I lie down with the knowledge that it wasn't.
For all my good intentions
I make the same mistakes I've always made,
display the same old weaknesses,
succumb to the same old temptations –
a constant cycle of failure.

Why does it happen?
I just can't work it out,
for I want so much to be faithful,
yet somehow, before I know it, I find I've fallen again,
unable to do even my own will,
let alone God's.
It's as though there are two selves at war within me,
one intent on good and the other on evil,
and you don't need me to tell you which one emerges the victor.
Can it ever change?
I'd like to think so,
but I honestly don't think it will,
for though the spirit is willing, the flesh is weak,
rushing, like a moth before a candle,
towards its own destruction.
Do you wonder that I despair sometimes?
It's impossible not to.
Yet I shouldn't lose heart,
because despite it all God still loves me,
not for what one day I might be,
but for what I am now,
with all my sin sticking to me.
That's why he sent his Son into the world –
not to save the righteous,
but to rescue people like you and me,
weak, foolish, faithless,
unable to help ourselves.
It doesn't mean I'll stop trying,
I'll never do that until my dying day.
But it *does* mean, however many times I fail,
however often he finds me lying in the gutter,
he'll be there to pick me up and set me on my way again,
cleansed, restored, forgiven,
the slate wiped clean, ready to start afresh –
through his grace, a new creation!

Prayer

Merciful God,
thank you that, unlike us, you don't dwell on our failures,
inviting us instead to acknowledge them openly before you,
to receive your pardon
and then to move on.
Teach us to do just that –
to accept your offer for what it is, and,
rather than wallow in our guilt,
to rejoice in your mercy.
Help us not simply to *talk* about new life but to *live* it joyfully,
receiving each moment as your gracious gift.
Amen.

Costly commitment

31

Did we know God would save us?

Shadrach, Meshach and Abednego

Then Nebuchadnezzar in furious rage commanded that Shadrach, Meshach and Abednego be brought in; so they brought those men before the king. Nebuchadnezzar said to them, 'Is it true, O Shadrach, Meshach, and Abednego, that you do not serve my gods and you do not worship the golden statue that I have set up?' Now if you are ready when you hear the sound of the horn, pipe, lyre, trigon, harp, drum, and entire musical ensemble to fall down and worship the statue that I have made, well and good. But if you do not worship, you shall immediately be thrown into a furnace of blazing fire, and who is the god that will deliver you out of my hands?' Shadrach, Meshach and Abednego answered the king, 'O Nebuchadnezzar, we have no need to present a defence to you in this matter. If our God whom we serve is able to deliver us from the furnace of blazing fire and out of your hand, O king, let him deliver us. But if not, be it known to you, O king, that we will not serve your gods and we will not worship the golden statue that you have set up.'

Daniel 3:13–18

Meditation

Did we know God would save us,
that whatever we faced he would see us through,
safe to the other side?
Well, no, we didn't actually, despite what some may tell you.
We wish we had done, for we'd have felt a whole lot happier,
ready to take whatever the king might throw at us.
But there were no guarantees, no cast-iron certainties –
we had to wait, and trust, and hope.
Of course he *could* deliver us,
but *would* he?
Who could say?
After all, why bother with us?
We were nobody special,
just three young men from Judah,
and though Nebuchadnezzar had singled us out for special treatment,

it didn't mean God had done the same.
We wouldn't be the first people to die for their faith,
or the last.
Yet at the time that wasn't our chief concern –
our faith was on the line,
our freedom,
our integrity,
our identity as a nation hanging in the balance,
and we had the chance to tip the scales.
It wouldn't have taken much to toe the line,
just a quick bow and it would all have been over –
surely not too awful a pill to swallow?
But what then,
what would happen the next time,
and the time after,
when the challenge came again?
First one compromise, then another,
and before long there'd be nothing left,
our lives bought at the cost of our souls.
So we stood firm,
hoping when it came to it he'd see reason,
respect our consciences,
honour our principles –
but we were wrong,
for he showed not even a glimmer of compassion
as he sent us off to our deaths.
I can't describe the heat of that furnace,
enough to knock you over before you even got close,
and as they thrust us towards it, we cowered in terror,
hope all but gone.
There was still time, of course,
time for God to step in and save us –
a last-minute reprieve,
stay of execution.
We knew he *could* do it, but *would* he?
And then they opened the door and hurled us in,
guards collapsing in agony as the heat overwhelmed them,
and we thought it was all over,
three more martyrs, soon forgotten.
Only it wasn't three;
there were four of us, and we were alive,

walking unharmed in the fire,
not even a hair on our heads singed by flames.
You think Nebuchadnezzar was puzzled by what he saw?
He wasn't the only one!
But then the truth dawned as our words came back to us:
'our God is able to deliver us from the fiery furnace'.
That's what we'd claimed,
that's what we hoped,
and that's what we found.
We knew he *could* do it –
we knew now he *had*!

Prayer

Sovereign God,
thank you for those who, in the face of persecution and danger,
have had the courage to stand up for their faith;
those whose dedication to you
has been an inspiration and example to others.
Thank you that today we are free to worship as we please,
without any need for fear or secrecy.
But, above all, thank you for the assurance that,
whatever we may face,
whatever dangers may threaten us,
you are able to deliver us from evil.
In life and in death you are by our side,
so that finally nothing will be able to separate us from your love.
Help us, then, to offer you our heartfelt worship,
and to honour you each day with faithful service.
Amen.

32

Do as you would be done by

A listener to Jesus

'Do to others as you would have them do to you . . . the measure you give will be the measure you get back.'

Luke 6:31, 38b

Meditation

Do as you would be done by.
Now *that's* an idea I can get my head round,
one that I'm more than happy to follow.
None of that 'love your enemies' stuff,
'turn the other cheek',
'give to those who beg' –
just sound commonsense advice.
It's what most of us do anyway, isn't it?
Treat people fair and they'll be fair with you.
Only, can it be quite so simple?
For he wasn't finished,
returning instead to the old bandwagon:
forgive,
judge not,
do good to all,
as though those are part of the same thought,
each belonging together.
He was right, of course,
for that's how I'd want others to treat me.
I'd expect them to make allowances when I wrong them,
to forgive and forget if I'm truly sorry.
I'd look for understanding of my actions,
a fair hearing rather than jumping to conclusions,
condemning out of hand.
And, should I be in need,

I'd hope for kindness,
help,
support.
Yet how many times, if I'm honest,
have I nursed a grievance,
leapt to pass judgement
and ignored the needy –
thinking only of myself?
I do it all the time,
loving where I'm loved,
giving as I receive,
my reaction towards others depending on *theirs* towards me.
'Do to others as you would have them do to you':
it sounds so straightforward,
so sensible,
but, taken seriously, it's harder than it sounds.
So often we do, not as we *would* be done by,
but as we *have* been –
and there's a world of difference between the two.

Prayer

Forgive, Lord, our knee-jerk reactions to others,
our instinctive desire to extract an eye for an eye
and a tooth for a tooth.
Forgive us for failing to see in ourselves
the wrongs we see in them;
for expecting allowances to be made for our faults
yet refusing to make them in turn.
Help us truly to do to others what we'd have done to us,
giving though we do not receive,
loving though no love is returned,
remembering that for us who deserve so little
you gave so much.
Amen.

33

We were puzzled, I don't mind telling you

The Apostle John

'Woe to you when all speak well of you, for that is what their ancestors did to the false prophets.'

Luke 6:26

Meditation

We were puzzled, I don't mind telling you,
for why should we be concerned instead of pleased
when people think well of us?
Surely if we live up to what Jesus asks of us,
loving our enemies,
responding to those in need,
we're bound to create a good impression?
Well perhaps,
perhaps not,
for truly following Jesus involves rather more.
It means rejecting the way of the world,
refusing to conform.
It means speaking the truth in love,
even though the truth may hurt.
It means speaking out against evil,
and standing up for what we believe.
All this,
and much more,
can be harder than we might think,
costing us money,
comfort,
opportunities,
friends.
Far easier to go along with the crowd,
compromise our convictions,
water down our faith.
And that's what false prophets did and continue to do,

telling people what they want to hear,
seeking approval at the cost of truth.
Yes, true faith will win its admirers,
but it will win its cynics too,
its mockers,
its enemies,
just as Jesus found,
and much though you might wish it were otherwise,
if you've never encountered something of those
then it's time to ask whether the faith you profess
is really faith at all.

Prayer

Living Lord,
though faith in you arouses scorn,
though serving you involves sacrifice,
though commitment to you meets with hostility
and though honouring you proves demanding,
help us to stay true to you,
faithful to our calling whatever life may bring.
Amen.

34

I couldn't get it at first

Peter

'Blessed are those who are persecuted for righteousness' sake, for theirs is the kingdom of heaven. Blessed are you when people revile you and persecute you and utter all kinds of evil against you falsely on my account. Rejoice and be glad, for your reward is great in heaven, for in the same way they persecuted the prophets who were before you.'

Matthew 5:10–12

Meditation

I couldn't get it at first.
What blessing can there be in persecution,
in facing hatred and hostility for the sake of Christ?
Okay, so they slandered the prophets before us,
hurling all kinds of insults against them,
but that doesn't make it good, does it? –
let alone something to be desired.
Surely there must be easier ways to secure heaven's rewards,
a less costly and demanding path?
What about those other things he mentioned,
like hungering and thirsting after righteousness?
Won't one of them do instead?
Maybe I'm not as meek and merciful as I should be,
as poor in spirit or pure in heart,
but I'm working on it
and will get there in the end.
But can any of those stand alone,
in splendid isolation from the rest?
There's the rub.
I want to say yes,
but his words suggest no,
everything he said and taught
speaking of distinctive commitment,
a way of life different from the world's,

challenging its norms and undermining the status quo.
In other words, true faith will ruffle feathers,
get under people's skin.
And that spells trouble,
for they won't like it –
won't like it at all,
and will silence us if they can,
just as they tried to silence him.
It's easier to keep your head down
to conform with the crowd and not ask awkward questions,
but from this question, at least, there's no running away.
I can stay in my comfort zone and leave others in theirs,
or I can stay true to Christ.
Sadly I can't do both.

Prayer

Living God,
give us, where necessary, the courage to be different,
to go against the expectations of the world
when they conflict with your truth, your way, your will.
Help us, as far as possible, to live peaceably with all,
never seeking confrontation or discord,
but aware also that there will be times when,
like those who have gone before us,
we must make a stand,
sticking up for the things we believe in,
even though that may entail facing scorn,
hostility,
rejection.
Inspire us through the life and witness of saints of old –
their faith, service and commitment –
to walk in their footsteps.
Save us from loving the world so much that we love you less,
from confusing the rewards of earth with the joys of heaven –
blessings you alone can give.
Amen.

35

Can you believe what he told us?

A listener to the Sermon on the Mount

'You have heard that it was said, "An eye for an eye and a tooth for a tooth." But I say to you, Do not resist an evildoer. But if anyone strikes you on the right cheek, turn the other also; and if anyone wants to sue you and take your coat, give your cloak as well; and if anyone forces you to go one mile, go also the second mile. Give to everyone who begs from you, and do not refuse anyone who wants to borrow from you. You have heard that it was said, "You shall love your neighbour and hate your enemy." But I say to you, Love your enemies and pray for those who persecute you, so that you may be children of your Father in heaven; for he makes his sun to rise on the evil and on the good, and sends rain on the righteous and on the unrighteous.'

Matthew 5:38–45

Meditation

Can you believe what he told us?
'Love your enemies,
pray for those who persecute you,
and if someone slaps you in the face, turn the other cheek!'
Well, I ask you, what sort of talk is that?
He's on another planet, this fellow –
cloud-cuckoo land!
Oh, it sounds wonderful, granted,
but can you see it working?
I can't.
No, we have to be sensible about these things,
realistic.
We'd all like the world to be different,
but it's no use pretending, is it?
'Love your enemies' –
where will that get us?
They'll see us coming a mile off!
And as for 'turn the other cheek' –
well, *you* can if you want to, but not me;

I'll give them one back with interest –
either that or run for it!
I'll tell you what, though,
we listened to him,
all of us,
just about the biggest crowd I've ever seen,
hanging on to his every word,
listening like I've rarely known people listen before.
Why?
Well, you could see he meant what he was saying for one thing –
the way he dealt with the hecklers and cynics:
never losing his cool,
never lashing out in frustration,
ready to suffer for his convictions if that's what it took.
He practised what he preached,
and there aren't many you can say that about, are there?
But it was more than that.
Like it or not, it was his message itself;
that crazy message,
so different from any we'd ever heard before –
impractical,
unworkable,
yet irresistible.
It gave us a glimpse of the way life could be,
the way it should be –
and he actually made us feel that one day it might be!
No, I'm not convinced, sad to say –
life's just not like that –
but I wish it was.
I wish I had the courage to try his way,
the faith to give it a go,
for we've been trying the way of the world
for as long as I can remember,
and look where *that's* got us!

Prayer

Lord,
we are told that the strongest survive,
that we need to look after number one,
that in this world it's a question of never mind the rest
so long as we're all right.
But you call us to another way:
the way of humility, sacrifice and self-denial,
of putting the interests of others before our own.
You stand accepted wisdom on its head,
claiming that the meek shall inherit the earth
and that those who are willing to lose their lives will truly find them.
Lord, it's hard to believe in this way of yours,
and harder still to live by it,
for it runs contrary to everything we know about human nature,
yet we have seen for ourselves what the world's way leads to.
Give us, then, faith and courage to live out the foolishness of the gospel,
and so to bring closer the kingdom of Christ here on earth.
Amen.

36

Even tax-collectors!

Matthew

'You have heard that it was said, "You shall love your neighbour and hate your enemy." But I say to you, Love your enemies and pray for those who persecute you, so that you may be children of your Father in heaven; for he makes his sun rise on the evil and on the good, and sends rain on the righteous and on the unrighteous. For if you love those who love you, what reward do you have? Do not even the tax-collectors do the same?'

Matthew 5:43–46

Meditation

Even tax-collectors!
What did he mean?
Was he having a dig at me or something?
For a moment I really thought so,
until he caught my eye and winked,
and I realised then it wasn't *me* he was teasing
but the crowd.
They thought they were so much better than I was,
chalk and cheese,
but he soon put them right,
showing that, at heart, we're all much the same.
We struggle to love, every one of us,
even what we feel for our nearest and dearest being flawed,
as much about *us* as anyone else.
That's the problem:
self gets in the way,
giving for what it can get,
expecting a *quid pro quo,*
and when that doesn't happen
our good intentions vanish on the breeze.
As for loving *others,*
those we don't get on with or who wish us ill:
forget it.

Yet that's what Jesus asked for,
and that's what he *did*:
loving people like me,
so-called tax-collectors and sinners;
loving *all*,
even those who nailed him to a cross;
loving both friends and enemies,
without reserve.
It was a hard way,
a costly way,
but it's the way that brought us life.
Lord, help me to love.

Prayer

Lord,
we *want* to love,
we *mean* to love,
we *try* to love,
but so often we fall short,
struggling to care for anyone but ourselves
and those closest to us.
Our fine intentions are sabotaged by greed,
pride,
envy,
resentment,
fear
and prejudice,
so that, time and again, we're found wanting.
Forgive us,
and help us to be channels of your love in Christ,
poured out so freely,
with no thought of the cost.
Flow in us,
and through us,
by his grace.
Amen.

37

Treasures on earth?

A listener to the Sermon on the Mount

'Do not store up for yourselves treasures on earth, where moth and rust consume and where thieves break in and steal; but store up for yourselves treasures in heaven, where neither moth nor rust consumes and where thieves do not break in and steal. For where your treasure is, there your heart will be also.'

Matthew 6:19–21

Meditation

Treasures on earth?
Huh, no chance of that!
It's all I can do to make ends meet,
so if Jesus thinks I'm likely to be snared by worldly wealth,
he's barking up the wrong tree.
Or is he?
For what, actually, do I most value,
enough to treasure it beyond all else?
If that's what he's asking, suddenly my answer is very different,
for, pressed to choose between heaven and earth,
I'm afraid the second too often wins.
I may talk of costly commitment, and so forth,
but my time, money and energy goes into serving self,
or, at least, my loved ones,
rather than God.
This world *matters* to me,
so much within it being special beyond words,
and *Jesus* believes that too, I'm sure of it.
Only he calls us to look deeper:
not simply to what enriches life,
but to what it's finally all about.
Put our hope in this world alone, he tells us,
confusing the gift with the giver,
creation with creator,

and our heart will inevitably be broken.
There *are* treasures on earth,
blessings to be received with thanks and joyfully celebrated,
but none of them, however precious, can satisfy our deepest need.
Only God can do that.

Prayer

Creator God,
help us to celebrate this world you have given us,
but not too much;
to enjoy the blessings of life,
but not to pin our happiness on them;
to make use of the abundant resources you have put at our disposal,
but not to abuse them.
Help us to remember that gratifying the body
is not the same as satisfying the soul;
that riches on earth are very different from treasures in heaven.
Teach us, then, to rejoice in all we have received now,
but to use it wisely, lovingly and responsibly,
setting our hearts above all on the things of your kingdom.
Amen.

38

'Ask,' he said, 'and you will receive'

A listener to the Sermon on the Mount

'Ask, and it will be given you; search, and you will find; knock, and the door will be opened for you. For everyone who asks receives, and everyone who searches finds, and for everyone who knocks, the door will be opened. Is there anyone among you who, if your child asks for bread, will give a stone? Or if the child asks for a fish, will give a snake? If you then, who are evil, know how to give good gifts to your children, how much more will your Father in heaven give good things to those who ask him!'

Matthew 7:7–11

Meditation

'Ask,' he said, 'and you will receive.'
Just like that,
or so at least it sounded.
As though all we have to do is put in our request,
place our order,
and at the drop of a hat it will be there before us,
served up on a plate,
exactly to our requirements.
Do you believe that?
I'm not sure *I* do.
And I'm not sure I want to either,
for if he really meant that,
then where would it all end,
when could we ever stop asking?
We couldn't, could we?
Not while there's still suffering in the world,
still need, sorrow, hunger, disease, despair.
It wouldn't be right –
a dereliction of duty, you might call it.
And anyway, even if we could wipe those out,
rid the world of its many ills,

that wouldn't be the end of it, not by a long way,
for there would always be something else to ask for –
a gift we know we lack,
a dream still unfulfilled,
a person we long to reach –
always just one more favour to call in
before we could be completely satisfied.
It would end up with God at our beck and call,
bowing to our every whim,
dancing to our tune instead of us responding to his.
So no, he couldn't have meant that, could he?
But what then?
What was Jesus getting at with that weird but wonderful promise?
I've wrestled with that puzzle day after day,
and I've begun to wonder if maybe we're looking at it
the wrong way round,
too much about self and too little about Jesus.
'Do not worry about your life,' he told us,
'what you will eat or what you will drink,
or about your body, what you will wear.
Strive first for the kingdom of God and his righteousness,
and all these things will be given to you as well.'
Ask for what matters, isn't that what he was saying –
for those things in life that can bring you lasting happiness –
treasures in heaven rather than pleasure on earth?
It's not that this life was unimportant to him.
He cared about the world's suffering more than anyone I've ever known.
But he came to tackle not simply the symptoms but the cause,
not just the way things look but the way they are –
the way we think, speak and act,
each transformed deep inside.
I may be wrong, of course,
but I think that's what he meant;
something like it anyway.
Ask God for guidance, strength, faith, renewal.
Ask him to teach, use, shape and forgive you.
Ask for such things,
earnestly,
honestly –
the gifts of his kingdom –
and you *will* receive until your cup runs over!

Prayer

Loving God,
you long to shower us with blessings,
to fill our lives with good things,
yet we frustrate your purpose and deprive ourselves
of the inexpressible riches you so freely offer.
We do not seek, so we do not find.
We do not ask, so we do not receive.
We concern ourselves with the fleeting pleasures of the moment
and so fail to grasp eternal treasures.
Forgive our shallow values and limited understanding,
and teach us to set our hearts on what can truly satisfy.
Amen.

39

It was a wonderful moment

Peter

He asked them, 'But who do you say that I am?' Peter answered him, 'You are the Messiah.' And he sternly ordered them not to tell anyone about him. Then he began to teach them that the Son of Man must undergo great suffering, and be rejected by the elders, the chief priests, and the scribes, and be killed, and after three days rise again. He said all this quite openly. And Peter took him aside and began to rebuke him.

Mark 8:29–32

Meditation

It was a wonderful moment:
I really thought I'd cracked it.
After all the uncertainty,
all the questions,
all the confusion,
I finally believed I understood who he was.
'You're the Messiah!' I told him,
and he beamed at me with such delight that I felt my heart would burst.
No one else had grasped it you see,
not properly.
They wondered, of course,
but like so many others they were still guessing,
groping in the dark.
He might as well have been Elijah or John for all they knew.
I was different, and Jesus knew it.
'Blessed are you,' he said,
'for God has revealed this to you and not man.'
What an accolade!
But then it all went wrong;
just when I felt I'd arrived, the bubble burst . . .
and with a vengeance!
I suppose I got carried away,
never stopped to think.

Typical of me, really.
It's just that it came as such a shock,
him going on like that about everything he had to suffer,
all doom and gloom,
even talking of death itself.
I wasn't having any of it.
'Not likely!' I shouted. 'No way!'
I meant no harm,
I just didn't think such things could happen to the Messiah,
But you should have seen his face:
the anger, the disappointment.
Satan, he called me!
Can you believe that?
Me, his right-hand man,
the one who'd just hit the nail on the head,
the pick of the bunch, so I thought –
Satan!
I was hurt at the time,
cut to the heart if I'm honest,
but I can see now, all too clearly, that he was right and I was wrong.
I still had so much to learn,
so much to understand,
and I needed a reprimand, a stern hand, if I was to progress any further.
I'd only just begun to glimpse the truth,
and if he'd done things my way
it would have meant him denying everything he stood for.
He *was* the Messiah,
but not in the way *I* meant it;
he *had* come to establish his kingdom,
but one very different from that which we expected.
His was the way of service, sacrifice and self-denial,
offering his life for the life of the world.
I see that now, and I marvel at his love,
but what I marvel at even more is that
even when I understood him so little
he understood me so much.

Prayer

Loving God,
thank you for milestones in our journey of faith –
moments when we have been especially conscious of your presence,
when faith has grown,
when truth has dawned on us in an unmistakable way.
Thank you for such times
but help us always to recognise that our journey is not ended
but only just begun.
Teach us that, however many answers we may have,
there is always more to see,
more to learn
and more to understand.
Amen.

40

Did those words of his hurt, you ask?

Peter

But turning and looking at his disciples, he rebuked Peter and said, 'Get behind me, Satan! For you are setting your mind not on divine things but on human things.'

Mark 8:33

Meditation

Did those words of his hurt, you ask?
Well yes, of course they did.
It's not every day someone calls you Satan.
And to be labelled such by your closest friend,
one you love and admire beyond all others –
understandably it leaves you shaken.
But let's be clear,
I deserved it, a hundred per cent,
for I should have known better.
It wasn't like he'd said anything new in warning us he must die.
He'd been utterly open about it from the start;
clear that he came not to lord it over us as the Romans did,
but to serve through sacrifice,
winning glory through humility,
triumph through defeat,
life through death.
Yet, I still couldn't get my head round that;
still saw success through human eyes rather than divine.
'You *can't* die!' I told him.
'You *mustn't*!'
Understandable, perhaps,
but wrong –
hideously, hopelessly wrong.
For if he didn't surrender his life,
choosing instead to serve self rather than others,
there would be no gospel to proclaim,

no Messiah to set us free.
I may have meant well,
but that wasn't enough,
the road to hell, as they say, being paved with good intentions.
I wanted joy without sorrow,
pleasure without pain,
answers that asked nothing of him
and still less of me,
and he helped me to realise that, for his kingdom to come,
there must necessarily be cost:
a price *he* would pay,
for us *all*.

Prayer

Lord Jesus Christ,
we struggle to come to terms with your way,
for it cuts across the norms and expectations of this world.
We resist the idea of surrendering all,
of losing our life in order to find it.
Like Peter, confronted by the stark reality of the cross,
we find ourselves asking:
isn't there a less costly, less demanding path?
Teach us the values of your kingdom,
where the last are first and the least greatest.
Teach us the meaning of love –
above all, of your love that fills the universe,
changing lives and transforming history.
Help us, then, for all our doubts and lack of understanding,
to celebrate what you have done,
and obediently to walk your way.
Amen.

41

Sheep among wolves

Luke

After this the Lord appointed seventy others and sent them on ahead of him in pairs to every town and place where he himself intended to go. He said to them, 'The harvest is plentiful, but the labourers are few; therefore ask the Lord of the harvest to send out labourers into his harvest. Go on your way. See, I am sending you out like lambs into the midst of wolves.'

Luke 10:1–3

Meditation

Sheep among wolves –
not much of a prospect, is it?
But give Jesus this,
he tells things straight,
honest to a fault.
He could have dressed things up,
pretended commitment is easy,
but he didn't,
leaving us instead under no illusions about what discipleship may cost.
Not that it's all doom and gloom.
We'll be encouraged sometimes,
our message welcomed,
but such moments will be the exception rather than the rule,
anomalies that buck the trend.
We don't like that idea, and it's hardly surprising,
for we want respect,
popularity,
success,
acclaim,
but such goals reflect *our* way of thinking
rather than *God's*.
If we're faithful to the gospel in word and deed,
witnessing through the people we are to the challenge of Christ,
then for every positive response we receive

there will be far more that are negative,
for every Yes, a string of Nos.
Don't lose heart, then, when the road is tough,
when commitment asks much yet seems to deliver little.
It's not an easy way to live,
but it's the *only* way to *life*.

Prayer

Lord Jesus Christ,
give us courage to walk your way,
even when it is demanding,
costly.
Help us stand up for our faith
and speak out for you,
resisting the temptation to go along with the world.
Remind us that though we may forfeit prosperity or popularity,
we will gain far more:
a life at one with you.
Amen.

42

We were on our own suddenly

Thaddaeus

These twelve Jesus sent out with the following instructions: 'Go nowhere among the Gentiles, and enter no town of the Samaritans, but go rather to the lost sheep of the house of Israel. As you go, proclaim the good news, "The kingdom of heaven has come near." Cure the sick, raise the dead, cleanse the lepers, cast out demons. You received without payment; give without payment.'

Matthew 10:5–8

Meditation

We were on our own suddenly,
sent out in the Master's name to proclaim the good news,
announce the dawn of his kingdom –
and it came as a rude awakening!
We'd been happy until then,
perfectly content to sit at his feet as he talked,
just the twelve of us and him, comfortably ensconced together.
It was a delight to be part of his intimate circle,
one of his chosen disciples.
and, given the choice, we'd have stayed listening to him for ever,
his words a constant source of inspiration,
his company a pleasure to share.
Only that was then, and this was now.
Suddenly the easy life was over
and it was time for us to play our part.
He wanted us to go out with the message he brought,
to share in his mission,
even one day carry it on ourselves;
and the picture he painted of what we could expect seemed very bleak,
not a prospect we welcomed at all.
Like sheep among wolves, he called it,
and out there, in the thick of things,
we soon realised what he meant –

the demands,
the pressures,
the corruption,
the hostility
utterly bewildering,
pressing in upon us until we didn't know where to turn next,
shattering our illusions,
sapping our strength,
battering our convictions –
honestly, I don't know how he coped.
We were glad to get back to him, I can tell you,
glad to lick our wounds and take shelter under his wings.
Yet we knew it couldn't last –
the time would come,
sooner rather than later,
when we had to go back and face the world again.
No good hiding your lamp under a bushel, he told us.
It must bring light to others, or else what use is it to anyone?'
He was right, of course,
but we still hoped it could wait a while,
just a little longer until we were ready.
You feel the same, do you?
I'm not surprised,
for it's easy to serve him when you're among friends –
so much harder when the world seems against you;
easy to trust when there's nothing asked of you –
so very different when it actually starts to cost.
Yet that's why he called us;
that's what it means to follow Jesus –
not simply to come *to* him but to go *for* him,
to show the reality of our faith through serving others,
find our life through losing it.
It's a costly business, there's no denying it,
the demands sometimes overwhelming, just as he said they would be,
but he's not asking from us any more than he gave himself,
for he offered everything, even life itself,
convinced that though the price may be high,
the rewards are higher,
and if that was enough for Jesus,
then, scared though I may be, it's enough for me.

Prayer

Lord Jesus Christ,
you do not simply call us to *believe* the good news;
you call us to *share* it.
Forgive us for all too often failing to do that.
We have been happy to *come* to you
but reluctant to *go out* in your name,
afraid of what might be asked of us
and unsure of our ability to respond to the challenge.
Help us to understand that discipleship without service
is no discipleship at all,
and that faith without witness
is a denial of the gospel we claim to believe.
Teach us, then, not only to rejoice in the love you have shown us
but, through word and deed, to share it with those around us.
Amen.

43

Take no copper in your belts

Matthew

'Take no gold, or silver, or copper in your belts, no bag for your journey, or two tunics, or sandals, or a staff; for labourers deserve their food.'

Matthew 10:9, 10

Meditation

Take no copper in your belts,
no bag for your journey,
no spare tunic, sandals or a staff.
Could he be serious, I wondered?
Surely not!
But he *was* –
we were to travel in faith,
confident that somewhere, somehow,
our needs would be met.
Well, my heart sank, you can imagine –
to set off on a journey not knowing where the next meal is coming from,
without a shekel to your name,
not to mention a change of clothing,
that takes some doing, believe me!
He was right, though, I came to see that later,
for it taught us not simply to live by faith,
important though that can be,
but to sort out our priorities
and to travel light.
You see, we couldn't have gone far with a load on our backs,
a sackful of provisions.
We had to be free,
unencumbered,
able to stride out wherever he might lead us –
and that's what we did,
not just then, but later,
going out in his name to proclaim his word.

Yet that's not the end of it,
for those words of his were not simply for us but for you,
as much about *your* journey as any.
'Do not worry about what you will eat, drink, wear,' he had said,
'but seek first the kingdom of God and his righteousness
and you will receive all these as well.'
'Sell everything, and give to the poor;
then come, follow me.'
'Come to me all you who are tired of carrying heavy loads
and I will give you rest –
take my yoke on you and learn from me,
for my yoke is easy
and my burden is light.'
In other words, let go of everything that binds us to earth,
that weighs us down and holds us back:
the grasping for riches and clinging to possessions
that consumes not just so much of our time but *us* as well,
leaving us empty instead of full,
hungry instead of satisfied.
Focus instead on the things that matter,
the resources he provides,
the true essentials of life.
I'm not telling you what to take for your journey –
that's between you and him –
but don't confuse what you want with what you need,
what will see you through with what will hold you back,
or else, far from being ready to travel
you may find yourself ready to drop,
and with nothing and no one to pick you up.

Prayer

Forgive us, Lord,
for our hearts lie too much with the things of this world,
on material possessions and earthly goals.
They bring us pleasure for a time,
but ultimately offer fleeting contentment rather than true satisfaction,
holding us captive rather than setting us free.
Though we try to pretend otherwise,
studiously avoiding the truth,
we cannot deny the inner emptiness that you alone can fill.

Help us, then, to seek,
before all else,
your kingdom and righteousness –
to let go of whatever weighs us down,
so that we may run the race you have set before us,
faithfully,
to the very end.
Amen.

44

We all have our cross to bear

Peter

'Whoever does not take up the cross and follow me is not worthy of me.'

Matthew 10:38

Meditation

We all have our cross to bear,
isn't that what they say?
Whatever it may be,
we all wrestle with some trouble or other.
So is that what Jesus means by those words of his?
No, it has to be more than that,
for the cross he has in mind seems to be shouldered *voluntarily*,
willingly and knowingly embraced.
So what *does* he mean?
You'd almost think he has crucifixion in mind –
as though he might someday have to pay the ultimate price.
But that's ridiculous, isn't it?
For surely he's sent by God,
the one long promised who will establish his kingdom
and set us free at last.
He's come to reign,
not to die;
to triumph over evil,
not suffer at its hands.
It has to be a figure of speech that stuff about a cross,
for I've seen all too many strung up over the years,
life draining excruciatingly away
until they beg for somebody to end it,
writhing in agony like a rag doll,
and, take it from me, it's not a pretty sight,
not pretty at all.
No, he must mean something different,
for no one would choose to face such horror –

not even Jesus.
Special he may be,
but could anyone be unique enough not only to give his life
but to inspire *me* to do the same?

Prayer

Saviour Christ,
for all our talk of costly discipleship,
walking the way of the cross,
when even small sacrifices are asked of us
we baulk at the prospect,
making excuses to avoid or water down your call.
We are reluctant to give a little,
let alone contemplate anything amounting to real sacrifice.
Forgive the feebleness of our faith,
our weak and feeble commitment,
and help us to follow you more faithfully,
if not to the cross
then at least to denying ourselves for the sake of others
and of you.
Amen.

45

'Teacher,' I said, 'what must I do to inherit eternal life?'

The lawyer who questioned Jesus

Just then a lawyer stood up to test Jesus. 'Teacher,' he said, 'what must I do to inherit eternal life?' He said to him, 'What is written in the law? What do you read there?' He answered, 'You shall love the Lord your God with all your heart, and with all your soul, and with all your strength, and with all your mind; and your neighbour as yourself.' And he said to him, 'You have given the right answer; do this, and you will live.' But wanting to justify himself, he asked Jesus, 'And who is my neighbour?' Jesus replied, 'A man was going down from Jerusalem to Jericho, and fell into the hands of robbers, who stripped him, beat him, and went away, leaving him half dead. Now by chance a priest was going down that road; and when he saw him, he passed by on the other side. So likewise a Levite, when he came to the place and saw him, passed by on the other side. But a Samaritan while travelling came near him; and when he saw him, he was moved with pity. He went to him and bandaged his wounds, having poured oil and wine on them. Then he put him on his own animal, brought him to an inn, and took care of him.'

Luke 10:25–34

Meditation

'Teacher,' I said, 'what must I do to inherit eternal life?'
and I knew what he was going to say,
even as I put the question.
It was typical of the man's genius,
somehow always turning the tables
on those who tried to catch him out.
And this time was no exception.
'What is written in the Law?' he asked.
'What do you read there?'
Brilliant!
Only this time he would meet his match,
for, unlike others, I was ready for him,

all set to turn the tables back again
and put him firmly on the spot.
So I played along, confident of emerging on top.
'Love God,' I said, 'and love your neighbour.'
It was the answer he'd been looking for,
and he nodded with a smile of satisfaction,
as though that was that,
the discussion at an end,
the issue resolved:
'Do this and you will live.'
But that was my cue,
and I leapt in gleefully,
sensing the kill.
'Yes,' I smirked, 'but who is my neighbour?'
Clever, don't you think?
And I genuinely believed I had him stumped,
one masterly stroke exposing the fatal flaw in his reasoning.
You see it sounds reasonable enough, doesn't it –
'Love your neighbour as yourself' –
the sort of commandment none of us would want to argue with,
never even presume to question;
but what does it actually mean?
If you've never asked yourself that then it's high time you did,
for perhaps then you'd be a little less keen on the idea,
a little less prone to let the words trip so lightly off the tongue.
Why?
Well, quite simply, how wide do you spread the net?
How far do you go before finally drawing the line?
The people next door, are they your neighbours?
Or is it those in your street,
your town,
your country
and beyond?
Where does it start?
Where does it end?
You tell me.
And that's the question I put to Jesus,
fully expecting him to flounder
as he tried to extricate himself from my trap.
Come on, I reasoned, there have to be limits somewhere!
The Romans, for example,

our hated oppressors –
he couldn't mean them for a start.
Nor tax-collectors, prostitutes and sinners,
you could write them off for certain –
accept *them* and we'd be talking of Samaritans next, God forbid!
So how about our enemies,
those who persecute, insult and accuse us falsely –
don't tell me we're meant to love them too?
Preposterous!
No, I had him pinned down,
his back to the wall,
and there could surely be no escape?
Only then he looked at me,
and told that unforgettable story about . . .
you've guessed it . . . a *Samaritan*! –
and somehow the question was once again back where it started,
with *me*:
'Which of these three was a neighbour to the man?'
I realised then with a stab of shock
and a sense of disbelief,
that he meant it,
that he seriously wants us to treat everyone, everywhere,
as our neighbour –
Jew and Gentile,
slave and free,
male and female,
rich and poor –
no person outside our concern,
no situation we can wash our hands of.
I'd put the question,
I had my answer,
and, I tell you what,
I wish I'd never asked!

Prayer

Lord Jesus Christ.
we feel overwhelmed sometimes
when we realise what you are asking of us,
when we begin to reflect on what is involved in Christian discipleship.
Your words about love for our neighbour sound wonderful
until we stop to ask what they mean,
and then, suddenly, the scale of the challenge,
the enormity of our responsibility
and the likely cost of service dawn on us
and we wonder how we can ever cope.
Fill us with your love so that we may love in turn.
Give us your spirit of humility and self-sacrifice,
and equip us to reach out in your name,
putting others before ourselves.
Teach us what it means to belong not just to the community of faith
but to the family of humankind,
and in serving there may we serve you also.
Amen.

46

He didn't mean me, I decided

A listener to Jesus

Someone in the crowd said to him, 'Teacher, tell my brother to divide the family inheritance with me.' But he said to him, 'Friend, who set me to be a judge or arbitrator over you?' And he said to them, 'Take care! Be on your guard against all kinds of greed; for one's life does not consist in the abundance of possessions.'

Luke 12:13–15

Meditation

He didn't mean me, I decided.
Well, he couldn't do, could he,
for I wasn't rich,
not by a mile,
and though I wouldn't have minded a bit extra in my pocket,
the occasional luxury at home,
I could hardly be termed greedy either.
No, he must have had others in mind,
people who are always after more –
you know the sort I mean.
Only I thought afterwards about what he'd said,
about there being more than one type of greed,
and suddenly I wasn't so sure he didn't meant me after all,
for I'm greedy in all kinds of ways –
for happiness, security, success and comfort to name but some –
and though there's nothing wrong with those in themselves,
there is if we try to turn them into possessions,
as though we can cling hold to them,
make them our own.
We just can't do that,
not in this life,
and if we look for meaning in this world alone
it will surely slip from our grasp,
like sand running through our fingers.

On what is our life based?
That's the question he was asking.
The things of God,
or the things of earth?
We can possess much yet have nothing,
own little but have all.
True contentment is in God's hands;
whether we find it is in *ours*.

Prayer

Forgive us, Lord,
for we spend so much of our lives chasing after illusory happiness,
thirsting for what can never satisfy,
pursuing riches on earth rather than treasure in heaven.
Help us to grasp where true fulfilment lies,
and to recognise that if we work for the things of your kingdom
with even a fraction of the effort we put into gaining worldly wealth,
we will find contentment indeed.
Amen.

47

A purse that never wears out

One of the crowd listening to Jesus

'Do not be afraid, little flock, for it is your Father's good pleasure to give you the kingdom. Sell your possessions, and give alms. Make purses for yourselves that do not wear out, an unfailing treasure in heaven, where no thief comes near and no moth destroys. For where your treasure is, there your heart will be also.'

Luke 12:32–34

Meditation

A purse that never wears out –
now I like the sound of that!
Just imagine:
pop your hand in your pocket,
any time,
anywhere,
and there it is,
cash on the nail,
as much as you need.
This guy's really talking!
Only he isn't,
for his sums don't add up.
'Sell your possessions,' he says,
'and give alms.'
Well, I'm sorry, but that's no way to invest for the future.
You'll end up, more like, with nothing,
relying on alms yourself,
and we can't *all* do that, can we,
for who'd be left then to give?
So what's he saying?
Don't tell me:
it's about letting go, isn't it,
hanging loose to money and possessions;
about understanding what's of real value,

able to satisfy the soul;
and, most of all, about receiving through giving,
a generous heart compared to an avaricious spirit?
I was afraid you'd say that,
for though I can accept it happily enough in theory,
in practice it's another matter,
neither *my* way nor that of the world.
We want treasure now *and* later,
rewards in this life *and* the life to come,
our hearts torn between God and self,
heaven and earth,
both/and rather than *either/or*.
I'll give Jesus this:
he's put his finger on the problem.
But that's the easy part.
It needs us to change, deep within,
if we're to find the answer;
our hearts to be realigned,
turned around.
Can he see to that too?

Prayer

Loving Lord,
we mean to be generous,
but find it hard to let go;
we mean to respond to others,
but struggle to put *them* first, *self* second.
For all our talk of treasure in heaven
it's treasures on earth that consume us . . .
even as we consume them!
Work within us,
and overcome our greed.
Help us to see beyond the flesh to the spirit,
in a world where so many,
all too literally,
can barely keep body and soul together.
Amen.

48

'Hate their life in this world?'

Andrew

'Very truly, I tell you, unless a grain of wheat falls into the earth and dies, it remains just a single grain; but if it dies, it bears much fruit. Those who love their life lose it, and those who hate their life in this world will keep it for eternal life. Whoever serves me must follow me, and where I am, there will my servant be also. Whoever serves me, the Father will honour.'

John 12:24–26

Meditation

'Hate their life in this world'?
What does he mean by that?
It sounds so negative,
hardly a great advert for Christianity –
as though the main criterion for following Jesus
is to be so thoroughly disenchanted that you want to end it all!
He can't mean that, surely,
and I don't think he does,
for he's spoken repeatedly of the joy he brings,
the blessings he wants to bestow,
not just in some distant future,
but here and now.
I don't hate life in this world, that's for sure,
but I *do* hate certain aspects:
those things that wound, damage and destroy,
scarring relationships and demeaning people as objects
to be used, exploited, ignored.
And yes, I hate my own culpability in its hurt and heartache,
for none of us are whiter than white,
untarnished by such faults.
Is this what Jesus had in mind?
That we must renounce this life if it leads us astray?
That we must be ready to make sacrifices,
even perhaps the greatest sacrifice of all,

in order to confront what we know to be wrong
and make a stand for good?
I can make sense of that,
strive towards it,
though I can't help feeling it's an ideal,
always out of reach,
for who among us would utterly renounce self
for the sake of others,
surrendering all for their sake?
It would take incredible courage,
unparalleled love.
Could anyone, I wonder –
even Jesus –
show devotion such as that?

Prayer

God of all,
give us a proper perspective on life.
Help us to celebrate the good things you have given –
to rejoice in the beauty of this world
and the blessings you daily shower upon us.
But help us also to grieve over whatever scars your creation,
denying your love and thwarting your purpose.
Teach us to stand up against such things,
irrespective of the cost to us,
recognising that true fulfilment and our ultimate destiny lie
not here on earth
but in your eternal kingdom,
where, by your grace, we will savour life indeed for evermore.
Amen.

49

I thought he might be the one we were waiting for

Judas Iscariot

'Do not think that I have come to bring peace to the earth; I have not come to bring peace, but a sword. For I have come to set a man against his father, and a daughter against her mother, and a daughter-in-law against her mother-in-law; and one's foes will be members of one's own household. Whoever loves father or mother more than me is not worthy of me; and whoever loves son or daughter more than me is not worthy of me; and whoever does not take up the cross and follow me is not worthy of me. Those who find their life will lose it, and those who lose their life for my sake will find it.'

Matthew 10:34–39

Meditation

I thought he might be the one we were waiting for,
the Messiah promised of old,
coming at last to deliver his people.
The Prince of Peace, isn't that what the prophet called him?
And my heart had thrilled at the prospect –
to think that after years of oppression, hatred and cruelty
there might finally be harmony between the nations,
an end to violence and bloodshed,
divisions put aside once and for all.
Idealistic, I know,
even naïve some might call it,
but I dared to hope,
to actually believe that we might see a world at one with itself.
Yet has it happened?
Well, not as far as I can see.
In fact, quite the opposite, that's what troubles me.
I hate to say it,
but I'm starting to think I got it wrong about Jesus;
that he's not at all the man I thought he was.

Just look around and ask yourself one question:
what he's actually done?
For it seems to me it's not peace he's brought but division.
I see people day after day arguing about who he is,
what he's come for,
what he's doing.
I've seen families divided,
marriages broken,
friendships destroyed,
all because people can't agree.
And today, do you know what he told us to expect?
More of the same, that's what!
I couldn't believe it –
instead of having some strategy to counter such discord,
he tells us it has to be.
And as if that's not enough, the problem is getting worse.
There are some now openly hostile to Jesus,
and making no secret of their feelings,
to the point that I fear greatly for his safety.
It's his own fault.
He's got people's backs up once too often,
spoken out of turn when he should have kept quiet,
and there's really no telling where it might end.
He came to unite us, so I thought –
to usher in a new era of harmony and peace,
but it hasn't worked out that way,
his coming, if anything, adding to the problem.
For while some would do anything for him,
worshipping the ground he walks on,
others would stop at nothing to see him silenced,
once and for all.
Me? I don't know what to believe any more,
but if anyone believes Jesus can bring us peace,
they must be living in another world, that's all I can say,
for I can't see it coming in this one . . .
can *you*?

Prayer

Lord of all,
we long to see peace in our world,
but the disturbing truth is that faith itself often creates division.
We look at history,
and across the centuries we see a sorry catalogue of atrocities
in the name of religion.
We look at the Church,
and even today, despite all the efforts to build unity,
there is still suspicion among various factions,
sometimes to the point of outright hostility.
We know this shouldn't be,
and yet we know also that peace doesn't come easily,
and certainly not through papering over the cracks.
Help us, then, to work for peace in whatever ways we can,
but also to stay true to you, even when doing so proves costly.
Amen.

50

I thought I was rich

Zacchaeus

'The kingdom of heaven is like treasure hidden in a field, which someone found and hid; then in his joy he goes and sells all that he has and buys that field. Again, the kingdom of heaven is like a merchant in search of fine pearls; on finding one pearl of great value, he went out and sold all that he had and bought it.'

Matthew 13:44, 45

Meditation

I thought I was rich,
for I had everything that money could buy –
good food,
warm clothes,
nice house,
fine possessions –
in fact, any and every luxury that took my fancy.
Not many can say that, can they?
Was I thankful?
Of course I was,
for I know there were plenty who'd have given their right arm
to enjoy wealth such as I had,
more than happy to swap places with me, given the chance.
And yet something was missing,
for, despite it all, happiness eluded me.
I seemed rich,
but I wasn't –
my belly may have been full,
but my soul was empty;
my spirit forever restless,
groaning in frustration,
yearning for nourishment,
searching for a sense of purpose in a world seemingly devoid of meaning.

And that's how it might have stayed, had I not met Jesus;
had I not heard and seen his words and deeds.
He spoke of a new kind of kingdom,
new way of living,
new relationship with God,
and I could tell immediately these this was what I'd been looking for:
a priceless jewel beside which all my treasures
seemed like tawdry trinkets,
a pearl that I had to make mine.
It didn't come cheaply, mind you,
for though, in one sense, it cost me nothing,
in another it cost all,
my total commitment,
unswerving loyalty,
willingness to sacrifice anything and everything in the Master's cause.
Yet I did so gladly,
with a spring in my step and song in my heart,
for I'd discovered wealth unlike any I'd known before,
a joy and sense of purpose more precious than words can express.
I thought I had much,
yet I had so little,
until I met with Christ and glimpsed the kingdom,
and now, though the world counts me poor,
my life overflows,
my cup runs over,
my heart is full
and my spirit is at rest.
What more could anyone want!

Prayer

Lord Jesus Christ,
we have so much to celebrate,
so many reasons to give thanks,
for you have given us untold riches in this life and the next.
Each moment offers us blessings too many to number –
a world of infinite beauty,
life full of inexhaustible fascination,
and your love overflowing with inexpressible grace.
Yet, somehow, despite it all, we lose our way,
failing to appreciate what we have received

and craving instead the riches of this world.
We hunger for material possessions,
thirst for the trappings of success
believe money can buy us happiness,
much though we try to deny it.
Forgive us the narrowness of our horizons,
and help us to grasp that true wealth lies in offering our lives to you
and surrendering ourselves in the service of others.
Teach us to share from our plenty,
to give without counting the cost,
to offer without seeking reward
even as you have offered everything for us.
So may we discover the awesome treasure of your kingdom,
the generosity of your love,
and the new life you extend freely to all.
Amen.

51

I thought I had everything under control

A wealthy listener to Jesus

Then he told them a parable: 'The land of a rich man produced abundantly. And he thought to himself, "What should I do, for I have no place to store my crops?" Then he said, "I will do this: I will pull down my barns and build larger ones, and there I will store all my grain and my goods. And I will say to my soul, 'Soul, you have ample goods laid up for many years; relax, eat, drink, be merry.'" But God said to him, "You fool! This very night your life is being demanded of you. And the things you have prepared, whose will they be?" So it is with those who store up treasures for themselves but are not rich toward God.'

Luke 12:16–21

Meditation

I thought I had everything under control,
the future mapped out exactly as I wanted it to be.
At long last I could sit back and enjoy life,
spoil myself a little,
indulge in the hard-won fruits of my labours.
And why not?
I'd earned it, hadn't I?
Those long years of striving,
the toil and effort to achieve success –
surely now I had a right to eat, drink and be merry?
Only that's when Jesus blew it all apart!
One simple story
and my blissful vision was exposed for what it was:
an empty illusion.
It's not that pleasures are wrong in themselves,
he wasn't saying that;
on the contrary, he enjoyed them as much as any,
his ministry in many ways being a celebration of life.
No, it was the way I viewed such things that was wrong:
as though they were *my* possessions,

for *my* use,
my benefit.
I'd put all my energy into self,
into securing my own happiness and fulfilment,
yet he showed me that all the things I pinned my faith on
hung by a thread that could be severed at any time.
Where then would all my toil have got me?
A lifetime sacrificed on the altar of ambition,
frittered away in the pursuit of gain.
Is that you, too?
Then listen again to those words of Jesus and let them speak to you.
Secure riches, by all means,
but don't keep them to yourself.
Use them to bring help to those in need,
hope to the poor,
food for the hungry.
Share with those who have little,
remembering that you have received so much.
Rejoice in what God has given by giving back to him in return.
Do that and you will discover the secret of true riches.
I'd lost sight of that,
blinded by treasures on earth to treasures in heaven,
but it's not too late,
for, with his help, I can change,
discovering where life's priorities really lie.
It's time to think of others;
time to think of God.

Prayer

Lord Jesus Christ,
we know that true riches do not lie on earth
and yet we find it hard to accept that fact.
Day after day, we strive to put a bit of extra money into our pockets,
longing for that unexpected windfall that will solve all our problems.
To splash out a little,
to treat ourselves to those few extra luxuries,
to afford our dream holiday, car or home –
these are the goals that dominate our thoughts
rather than the pursuit of treasure in heaven.
We struggle to see beyond the allure of material pleasures,

even though we know the satisfaction they offer is often illusory,
unable to satisfy our deepest needs.
Open our eyes to true riches:
to the blessings and fulfilment you alone can offer,
and the priceless inheritance of your kingdom.
Amen.

52

'Hate father and mother!'

Mary, mother of Jesus

Now large crowds were travelling with him; and he turned and said to them, 'Whoever comes to me and does not hate father and mother, wife and children, brothers and sisters, yes, and even life itself, cannot be my disciple.'

Luke 14:25, 26

Meditation

'Hate father and mother'!
What can he mean?
For he doesn't hate *me*, that's for sure.
He may seem curt, sometimes,
even cold,
for he's preoccupied by the burden of ministry –
the demands,
the pressure,
the cost –
but he cares about my welfare as much as any son cares for his mum,
and more besides.
So what's this talk of his, so stark and shocking?
I don't understand.
But wait . . .
perhaps I do . . .
for both Joseph and I saw early on that nothing –
nothing at all –
would deflect him from his calling;
that if it was a choice between serving us or God,
then God would always win.
He wouldn't oppose us if he could help it,
still less cause unhappiness,
but if we or anyone else stood in the way of right,
of what he believed must be done,
then he would make a stand, come what may.

That's what he means, surely:
not that we should *hate* anyone
but that we must love God more than all,
putting him even before those we hold most dear
if serving *them* means betraying *him*.
It's a question of what matters most,
where our ultimate allegiance lies,
and whether, if – God forbid – you're put to the test,
you'll take the easy way,
or the hard.

Prayer

Teach us, Lord, to love others,
but none too much;
to seek the good of those we hold dear,
but never to put them before you.
Help us to be true in all our relationships,
but to recognise when we must choose between them and you,
lest we end up betraying all.
Amen.

53

I had to pinch myself for a moment

One in the crowd who followed Jesus

'For which of you, intending to build a tower, does not first sit down and estimate the cost, to see whether he has enough to complete it? Otherwise, when he has laid a foundation and is not able to finish, all who see it will begin to ridicule him, saying, "This fellow began to build and was not able to finish." Or what king, going out to wage war against another king, will not sit down first and consider whether he is able with ten thousand to oppose the one who comes against him with twenty thousand? If he cannot, then, while the other is still far away, he sends a delegation and asks for the terms of peace. So therefore, none of you can become my disciple if you do not give up all your possessions.'

Luke 14:28–33

Meditation

I had to pinch myself for a moment.
Was I hearing the man rightly?
The promised Messiah, some were calling him,
God's chosen one.
So I'd come to see for myself –
and one thing was for sure,
he was unlike any of those who'd claimed that title before.
Follow *me*, was the usual line,
and life will be better than you've ever known it,
your hopes realised,
dreams fulfilled,
everything as you've always wanted it to be.
No suggestion of problems along the way,
no minus side to balance the plus –
it was always the proverbial bed of roses,
a land flowing with milk and honey and not a bitter herb in sight.
And the astonishing thing is that people swallowed it,
time and again responding in their droves,
only to find those much-vaunted dreams laid waste,

wild promises exposed for the sham they were.
You couldn't say that of Jesus, though,
not for a moment.
There was no hard sell,
no dressing things up or pulling the wool over our eyes.
He laid it on the line,
straight down the middle,
the cost of commitment crystal clear.
If anything you'd have thought he was trying to put people off
rather than canvass recruits.
Oh, there'd be blessings too, he was clear on that,
treasures in heaven for those with the courage to follow,
but even these involved sacrifice,
real, painful sacrifice that many would find hard to bear,
and that would call for every ounce of allegiance,
testing faith to the limit.
He offered much –
the gateway to life,
path to eternal fulfilment –
but he left us under no illusions,
The road is rough and the journey hard,
involving, finally, the way of the cross.
Have we the courage to walk it?

Prayer

Lord Jesus Christ,
we find it hard enough to give up *anything*,
let alone *everything*!
Though we extol the virtues of self-sacrifice,
we live by the creed of self-interest,
what we give to you and others being measured by what we can afford
after we have first taken care of ourselves.
We try to fool ourselves that we are not tied to our possessions,
that we could leave them all behind without a moment's compunction,
but we know in our hearts that the reality is different –
that we would cling to them tenaciously
should our hold on them ever be threatened.
Despite the stranglehold they exercise over our lives,
we cannot find sufficient courage to abandon the values of this world
and embrace those of your kingdom.

Move within us, we ask,
and give us a new heart and spirit,
a mind at peace
and a life liberated in your service.
Amen.

54

I should have learnt, shouldn't I?

Peter

From that time on, Jesus began to show his disciples that he must go to Jerusalem and undergo great suffering at the hands of the elders and chief priests and scribes, and be killed, and on the third day be raised. And Peter took him aside and began to rebuke him, saying, 'God forbid it, Lord! This must never happen to you.' But he turned and said to Peter, 'Get behind me, Satan! You are a stumbling block to me; for you are setting your mind not on divine things but on human things.'

Matthew 16:21–23

Meditation

I should have learnt, shouldn't I? –
for that rebuke was devastating:
'Get behind me, Satan!'
Not that Jesus was angry, despite how it sounds –
more dismayed,
frustrated,
and hardly a surprise given the temptation he'd faced
and was facing still.
You see, he didn't relish suffering any more than the rest of us,
but he'd wrestled in the wilderness with that calling,
as he'd wrestle again in Gethsemane,
and knew there was no other way.
He had to carry the cross to bear our sins,
to die that we might live,
and the thought that *I* at least understood,
even if no one else did,
warmed his heart . . .
only for those impulsive words of mine to blow it all away.
I was mortified,
shame overcoming my hurt,
but would you believe it,
when the moment came and the soldiers closed in,

the spectre of his death drawing near,
I grabbed a sword and lunged at them,
denying his way to the last.
I'd failed to grasp the nature of his kingdom–
a kingdom in which success means sacrifice
and splendour involves service,
its king crowned with thorns via a cross.
Don't make my mistake,
judging the divine by the human,
things above by the world below.
However hard it may be,
however strange,
however contrary to logic and inclination,
you too must trust in him,
ready to lose *much* to receive *all*.

Prayer

Forgive us, Lord,
for eroding the message of the gospel,
blunting its challenge on the anvil of expediency,
self-interest and complacency.
We are swift to compromise when staying faithful
involves the prospect of cost.
We rebel when *your* way runs contrary to our own.
We close our minds to what upsets the status quo.
We resist your call when it poses awkward questions
that we'd rather not face.
Teach us to set our hearts on things of heaven
rather than those of earth;
to acknowledge you as Lord,
not only with our lips but also with our lives.
Amen.

55

What does he mean, 'dishonest wealth'?

A modern-day Christian

'Whoever is faithful in a very little is faithful also in much; and whoever is dishonest in a very little is dishonest also in much. If then you have not been faithful with the dishonest wealth, who will entrust to you the true riches? And if you have not been faithful with what belongs to another, who will give you what is your own? No slave can serve two masters; for a slave will either hate the one and love the other, or be devoted to the one and despise the other. You cannot serve God and wealth.'

Luke 16:10–13

Meditation

What does he mean, 'dishonest wealth'?
He's barking up the wrong tree there,
for my money has been fairly earned,
legal and above board.
Only it's not that simple, is it,
for who can say what deals it's financed,
palms greased,
services bought,
or wrongs contributed to?
It may seem innocent enough, the cash in my pocket
yet it's a dangerous thing,
to be handled with caution,
not necessarily the root of all evil in itself,
but soon becoming so should we love it too much.
And as I thought about those words of Jesus –
really thought –
I realised I do just that,
for I found myself increasingly uncomfortable,
trying to water down,
explain away,
what I'd rather not hear.
I talk of using my money wisely,

giving to those in need,
but more often than not my charity starts at home . . .
and stays there.
I talk of fair trade,
ethical investment,
yet far too frequently it's *all* talk and nothing more.
Time and again, as Jesus warned, I attempt to serve two masters,
and no prizes for guessing, when the two clash, which one wins.
I may *get* my money fairly,
but do I *use* it fairly as well?
That's the question.
The first is easy enough.
The second not easy at all.

Prayer

Forgive us, Lord,
for we are part of an unjust and unequal world,
a world in which we have plenty at the cost of others.
Help us to do what we can to redress the balance,
not just through giving to charity,
but through using our money wisely
so that it contributes towards change.
Though economic issues are complex
save us from hiding behind them;
from foolishly believing we can both have our cake and eat it,
serving *self* as well as you.
Amen.

56

It was a lot to ask, wasn't it?

The rich ruler

A certain ruler asked him, 'Good Teacher, what must I do to inherit eternal life?' Jesus said to him, 'Why do you call me good? No one is good but God alone. You know the commandments: "You shall not commit adultery; You shall not murder; You shall not steal; You shall not bear false witness; Honour your father and mother."' He replied, 'I have kept all these since my youth.' When Jesus heard this, he said to him, 'There is still one thing lacking. Sell all that you own and distribute the money to the poor, and you will have treasure in heaven; then come, follow me.' But when he heard this, he became sad; for he was very rich. Jesus looked at him and said, 'How hard it is for those who have wealth to enter the kingdom of God! Indeed, it is easier for a camel to go through the eye of a needle than for someone who is rich to enter the kingdom of God.'

Luke 18:18–25

Meditation

It was a lot to ask, wasn't it,
too much to expect of anyone?
I was ready to do my bit, after all,
happy to be more than generous if that's what he wanted;
but to give up everything,
to leave it all behind so that I could follow him –
well, quite simply, it wasn't on.
So I left,
disappointed,
disillusioned,
preferring riches I could handle now
to the promise of treasure in heaven.
It was a shame though –
had he asked for a quarter,
a half,
even the bulk of my wealth,
I'd have said yes, happily enough,
for he had something I didn't,

a tranquillity, assurance, sense of purpose beyond price,
more precious than anything money can buy,
and I wanted to share it,
to grasp hold of a prize that would never fade or perish.
Did I have my regrets?
Of course I did,
and I prayed many times for help to accept his challenge,
yet somehow, though I longed to respond,
the resolve was never quite there.
Until today, that is,
for I arrived here in Jerusalem for the Passover,
and I saw a crowd gathering in the streets,
and, there among them, a man struggling under a cross,
collapsing in exhaustion,
writhing in agony as they nailed him up to die.
And, do you know what?
It was Jesus.
Don't ask how it could happen, for I'll never know –
how anyone could kill a man like that just makes no sense –
yet I understood one thing.
He'd given his all,
everything,
precisely what he'd asked of *me*,
and more besides!
And suddenly,
as I watched him suffer,
as I heard his groans,
as I saw him take his final breath,
his words came flooding back,
cutting deep into my soul:
'Sell all that you own and distribute the money to the poor,
and you will have treasure in heaven;
then come, follow me.'
It wasn't much to ask, was it?

Prayer

Gracious God,
no one can ever give us more than you have given,
for you have blessed us with life in abundance,
overflowing with good things,
and to make that gift possible you gave of yourself,
not just a little but all.
You bore the limitations of our flesh;
you endured rejection, humiliation and finally death on a cross;
and, most awesome of all, through Christ you took on yourself
the dreadful burden of human sinfulness,
experiencing the despair and isolation that brings.
Forgive us that, despite all this, we give so grudgingly in return;
that though our words say one thing, our lives say another.
Forgive us that so often our thoughts are little for you,
none for others
and all for ourselves.
Help us to recognise afresh what you have done for us,
and to give something back in return.
Amen.

57

I've never been so embarrassed

The Apostle James

Then the mother of the sons of Zebedee came to him with her sons, and kneeling before him, she asked a favour of him. And he said to her, 'What do you want?' She said to him, 'Declare that these two sons of mine will sit, one at your right hand and one at your left, in your kingdom.' But Jesus answered, 'You do not know what you are asking. Are you able to drink the cup that I am about to drink?' They said to him, 'We are able.' He said to them, 'You will indeed drink my cup, but to sit at my right hand and at my left, this is not mine to grant, but it is for those for whom it has been prepared by my Father.' When the ten heard it, they were angry with the two brothers. But Jesus called them to him and said, 'You know that the rulers of the Gentiles lord it over them, and their great ones are tyrants over them. It will not be so among you; but whoever wishes to be great among you must be your servant, and whoever wishes to be first among you must be your slave.'

Matthew 20:20–27

Meditation

I've never been so embarrassed;
the way his face fell at our question
will be etched on my memory for ever.
Oh, he tried to let us down gently,
concerned for our feelings as always,
but I could tell he was disappointed in us,
dismayed that we should even have thought of asking.
To be fair, it was our mother's idea,
though we played along quite happily,
glad, in fact, she'd taken the initiative.
'Think of the future,' she told us.
'What's going to happen then?'
And she was genuinely troubled,
understandably so,
for we'd packed in our jobs,
left home, family, livelihood, everything

to follow Jesus,
and she wanted to know, quite simply, what was in it for us.
Yes, it may sound shabby now,
but at the time it seemed perfectly natural to ask.
After all, we'd no idea what the future might bring,
what demands would be made of us,
sacrifices expected,
so it seemed only fair to seek some guarantee of long-term security.
Remember, also, that we'd been the first to respond,
so why not be the first to benefit? –
it wasn't like we were jumping the queue.
Only that's not how the others saw it!
They were incensed,
more angry than I've ever seen them,
and as to the accusations they hurled at us,
well, they're best left unsaid.
But with Jesus it was different.
There was no anger from him,
no disgust at our request;
rather, if anything, anxiety, concern.
It was as though we were spoilt children
with no idea what we were asking –
and I'm afraid that just about sums it up.
We'd followed him,
listened to his words,
witnessed his deeds,
but we'd taken in precious little of what he'd tried to show.
We knew he was special,
the promised Messiah,
but we hadn't begun to understand what that meant.
Instead of serving *him*, we were serving *self*,
our own welfare, interests and future all that really mattered to us.
No wonder he shook his head,
for as he was later to show us so powerfully on the cross,
when it comes to his kingdom, the first will be last,
and the last, first.

Prayer

Lord Jesus Christ,
we want to serve you,
and like to believe we do,
but unwittingly we can turn even faith into serving ourselves.
We gain strength through fellowship and worship
but neglect your call to mission.
We focus on our own concerns in prayer
and forget about the world beyond.
We expect *you* to do *our* will,
rather than *us*, *yours*.
Even our deeds of kindness
can finally be more about our own sense of righteousness
than the needs of those we think we are serving.
Overcome the stranglehold of self
and help us to understand that true discipleship brings its own reward:
the joy of knowing and loving *you*.
Amen.

58

I was ashamed, if I'm truthful

The widow at the treasury

He looked up and saw rich people putting their gifts into the treasury; he also saw a poor widow put in two small copper coins. He said, 'Truly I tell you, this poor widow has put in more than all of them; for all of them have contributed out of their abundance, but she out of her poverty has put in all she had to live on.'

Luke 21:1–4

Meditation

I was ashamed, if I'm truthful,
desperately praying that no one would notice me,
for what would they think
when they saw those two miserable coins of mine;
what sort of person would they take me for?
They seemed little short of an insult,
worse, in some ways, than bringing nothing at all.
It had been different once,
when my husband was alive –
then I could hold my head up in any company,
my gifts, if not extravagant, being more than adequate.
But times were hard now,
and it was a matter of getting by as best I could;
not only life's little luxuries were a thing of the past,
but many of its necessities too.
Yet, even if it meant going short,
I was resolved to continue offering something to God.
So there I was, that day in the Temple,
surreptitiously bringing my feeble gift.
It wasn't much, I know,
not in the eyes of the world, anyway,
but to me it was a small fortune,
all I had left in the world.
Well, you can imagine my horror when I arrived there

to find this crowd with Jesus, watching.
It was my worst nightmare come true,
my pathetic offering exposed to the full glare of public scrutiny,
and I felt certain I would die of shame,
the colour rising to my cheeks,
skin crawling with embarrassment.
Yet Jesus singled me out, would you believe,
not as an object of ridicule but as an example to follow.
He understood that it's the thought that counts,
and somehow knew how much that gift had cost me –
to him those small pieces of copper being like nuggets of gold!
I went out that morning with my heart singing,
head held high after all,
and I brought whatever I could offer, from then on,
without any hesitation or sense of unworthiness,
for I understood that God sees things differently from us:
that he measures the gift not by how much it's worth,
but by how much it means!

Prayer

Gracious God,
you give to us out of love;
forgive us for so often giving back to you out of habit or duty,
or because our conscience pricks us.
Teach us instead to give joyfully,
not because we must but because we may;
to offer our money, worship and service as a gesture of love
and expression of our appreciation.
Help us to understand that it is not the gift that matters
so much as the spirit in which it is given,
and may that awareness inspire all we offer to you.
Amen.

59

This time I will not fail

Peter

Simon Peter, a servant and apostle of Jesus Christ, to those who have received a faith as precious as ours through the righteousness of our God and Saviour Jesus Christ: may grace and peace be yours in abundance in the knowledge of God and of Jesus our Lord. His divine power has given us everything needed for life and godliness, through the knowledge of him who called us by his own glory and goodness. Thus he has given us, through these things, his precious and very great promises, so that through them you may escape from the corruption that is in the world because of lust, and may become participants of the divine nature. Therefore, I intend to keep on reminding you of these things, though you know them already and are established in the truth that has come to you. I think it right, as long as I am in this body, to refresh your memory, since I know that my death will come soon, as indeed our Lord Jesus Christ has made clear to me. And I will make every effort so that after my departure you may be able at any time to recall these things.

2 Peter 1:1–4, 12–15

Meditation

This time I will not fail:
despite the terror,
the sorrow,
the pain,
I will not fail.
God knows I don't want to die –
I'm not the stuff of heroes,
but then I hardly need tell you that, do I?
You'll all know well enough about the last time.
It's been written about,
talked about,
preached about so many times –
Peter, the man who was all talk,
the apostle who lost his nerve when the pressure was on.
The memory has lived with me ever since,

searing into my conscience like a hot iron.
Not that Jesus didn't forgive me;
he soon put me right on that.
Three times he affirmed his call,
three times offered me the opportunity to declare my love,
one for each of my denials.
No, he never blamed me for my failure,
never condemned,
not even once the slightest hint of censure,
let alone telling me, 'I told you so.'
And to be fair, neither has anyone else.
They all understood I meant well,
knew equally how easily they'd have done the same;
and if anyone felt it served me right for shooting my mouth off
they never said.
Yet I've had to live with the knowledge of my empty promises,
my extravagant worthless claims;
and sometimes, I can tell you, my skin still crawls with shame.
It's as though, deep down, I don't believe I can trust myself,
and because of that I ask myself why anyone else should trust me either.
Well, now's the time to put the record straight,
here as I rot in jail waiting for the final moment
when the executioner comes,
when death finally arrives.
It won't be easy, I know that.
They'll push me to recant,
threaten me,
torture me,
maybe even promise life if I'm ready to to turn my back on Jesus
as I did all those years ago.
But not this time:
this time I will not fail.
I was given another chance to live,
forgiven,
restored,
accepted;
and I seized it with both hands,
living life to the full in a way I never lived it before.
Now I have another chance to die,
another chance to offer my life for the one who died for all,
and this time I will stay true to the end,
for I know that in death, as in life, he will stay true to me.

Prayer

Lord Jesus Christ,
you know that, despite our faith, we have repeatedly failed you.
The spirit is willing but the flesh is weak.
Yet however often we let you down,
you set us back on our feet,
offering us the chance to start afresh and make amends.
Help us to learn from our mistakes
and to walk more faithfully in your footsteps,
whatever it may cost.
Amen.

Examining ourselves

60

Who did he take me for?

Naaman

Naaman, though a mighty warrior, suffered from leprosy. Elisha sent a messenger to him, saying, 'Go, wash in the Jordan seven times, and your flesh shall be restored and you shall be clean.' But Naaman became angry and went away, saying, 'I thought that for me he would surely come out, and stand and call on the name of the Lord his God, and would wave his hand over the spot, and cure the leprosy! Are not Abana and Pharpar, the rivers of Damascus, better than all the waters of Israel? Could I not wash in them, and be clean?' He turned and went away in a rage. But his servants approached him and said to him, 'Father, if the prophet had commanded you to do something difficult, would you not have done it? How much more, when all he said to you was, "Wash, and be clean"?' So he went down and immersed himself seven times in the Jordan, according to the word of the man of God; his flesh was restored like the flesh of a young boy, and he was clean. Then he returned to the man of God, he and all his company; he came and stood before him and said, 'Now I know that there is no God in all the earth except in Israel.'

2 Kings 5:1a, c, 10–14

Meditation

Who did he take me for?
That's what I wanted to know!
Honestly, I wasn't just any old visitor,
one of his average clientele;
I was a national celebrity,
commander of the Aramean army,
accepted in the highest circles of the land.
And why not? –
for, against all the odds, I'd led them to victory,
distinguished myself both in leadership and valour.
So when this so-called prophet ordered me to take a dip in the Jordan,
quite frankly, I was livid.
It was an insult,
a deliberate attempt to humiliate me,

at least that's how it seemed –
and had I been back in my own country
I'd have clapped the fellow in irons
or had him flogged on the spot.
Not that I was surprised, mind you,
for I'd had my doubts from the beginning,
the moment that servant girl of mine
dreamt up the hair-brained scheme.
Oh, she meant well, no doubt,
and I was touched by her devotion;
but, I ask you: *Israel* – hardly the centre of the universe, is it?
So there I was, stomping back home in a rage,
telling myself I'd been a fool to listen to her,
when one of my men took me quietly aside.
It took some doing, tackling me in a mood like that,
and I could see he half expected me to bite his head off,
but even as the oaths were forming on my lips
so his words sunk home.
In all honesty, what had I to lose?
surely anything was better than the fate in store for me
if I failed to find a cure.
And let's face it, whether it be Aram or Judea,
a river is just a river.
It was my pride holding me back, nothing more,
a misplaced sense of my own importance preventing me
from taking perhaps the most important step of my life.
So I went down into the water,
just as he'd told me to;
and when I came up that seventh time,
it wasn't just my skin made new,
it was my mind,
my soul,
my everything –
life more precious than it had ever been before!
Who did he think he was?
That's what I asked at the beginning.
But as I made my way home,
I realised it was the wrong question,
to the wrong person,
for I'd been touched by that God of his –
a God unlike any I'd met before,

and a God who was asking me, quite simply,
who did *I* think *he* was?

Prayer

Gracious God,
you call us to walk humbly with you,
open to your voice and the voice of others,
yet too often we are full of our own importance.
We believe we know best,
and resent ideas different from our own.
We think we can cope,
and resist offers of support.
We talk of your glory,
but it is our own that concerns us.
Forgive us for looking inwards instead of outwards;
letting our preoccupation with self obscure your presence
and blind us to your will.
Teach us to humble ourselves under your mighty hand,
knowing that you alone can lift us up to life in all its fullness.
Amen.

61

He was full of surprises, that man

The woman at the well

A Samaritan woman came to draw water, and Jesus said to her, 'Give me a drink.' (His disciples had gone to the city to buy food.) The Samaritan woman said to him, 'How is it that you, a Jew, ask a drink of me, a woman of Samaria?' (Jews do not share things in common with Samaritans.)

John 4:7–9

Meditation

He was full of surprises, that man,
from the moment I first met him.
I thought he'd just push me aside like all the rest;
either that or walk away with his head in the air.
He was a Jew, remember, and I a Samaritan;
and worse than that,
a woman,
alone.
Yet he stayed where he was, a smile on his face,
quite happy, apparently, to be associated with me.
Well, call me suspicious if you like, but I wasn't sure what he was up to,
so I asked him straight out, 'What's your game?'
He laughed at that, and then offered me a drink of water –
at least I thought that's what he was doing, though I wasn't sure.
You see, he had no bucket,
and he could hardly shin down the well, could he?
So where was this water he was on about meant to come from?
To be frank, I suspected he was pulling my leg,
but I was beginning to like him despite the nonsense he talked.
He had a nice way with him,
kind,
gentle,
a bit of all right in an unconventional sort of way.
So I played along, wondering where it would all lead.
If only I'd known –

what an embarrassment I might have saved myself.
I'll never know how he guessed,
but suddenly he looked straight at me
and for the first time I noticed his eyes.
They didn't undress you like so many men's seem to do,
but looked much deeper,
almost as if into my very soul.
And then he started talking about my lovers,
my husbands,
my past,
every detail correct.
It was uncanny,
frightening,
far too near the knuckle,
So I tried to fob him off with some old chestnut about worship.
But even then he threw me;
none of the usual pat answers
but a response that reached right to the heart of the matter,
cutting through all the trivia.
And it was after this that he produced the biggest surprise of all –
told me he was the Messiah!
I didn't know what to say,
just stood there gawping, flabbergasted.
I mean, I realised he was a prophet,
but the Messiah?
It couldn't be, I told myself,
no way.
I went back down to the village, seeking reassurance,
wanting someone to tell me he was just another religious nutcase.
But they didn't.
They were curious,
wanted to see for themselves.
And when they heard him,
listened to his teaching,
they believed he was who he claimed to be:
the promised one of God.
You think that unlikely?
Well yes, *I* did too,
but I tell you again, he was full of surprises, that man,
the most amazing man I've ever met.
So, incredible or not, it may just possibly be true.

Prayer

Lord Jesus Christ,
we talk of following you
but much of the time we expect *you* to follow *us*.
Break through the chains we put around you
and help us to face the challenge you daily bring
if only we have eyes to see and ears to hear.
Amen.

62

'Your will be done, on earth as it is in heaven'

An early Christian

'Pray then in this way: Our Father in heaven, hallowed be your name. Your kingdom come. Your will be done, on earth as it is in heaven.'

Matthew 6:9, 10

Meditation

'Your will be done, on earth as it is in heaven.'
Yes, I know I said it, Lord,
but I didn't expect you to take me literally;
never imagined for a moment you'd hold me to the bargain.
Change the world by all means,
others too, come to that,
but me?
Can't you make an exception?
What I meant by 'Your will be done' was '*Let* it be your will',
not '*If* it be'.
Come on, Lord, be reasonable.
You know best, I realise that,
and of course your purpose comes first,
but surely you can work round me,
fit my requests into your plan somewhere?
That's not too much to ask, is it?
You know what I want from you,
how much it means to me –
don't go spoiling things, please.
What's that you say?
I've got things wrong,
my priorities muddled?
Now hang on, Lord,
I've said it once,
I'll say it again,

'Not your will but mine be done.'
Whoops, I got that wrong, didn't I?
Didn't I?

Prayer

Sovereign God,
we want to echo the words of Jesus:
'Not my will but yours be done',
but we find it so hard to put you first and self second.
Despite our promises of allegiance,
we expect you to accommodate our wishes and bow to our demands,
and, when you fail to deliver the goods,
we wonder why you have not answered our prayer.
We speak of seeking your guidance and discovering your purpose,
yet, more often than not, we trust in *our* judgement,
our minds already made up before we approach you.
Open our hearts to your presence
and give us humility to listen,
wisdom to understand
and faith to follow.
Help us to say, 'Your will be done',
and to mean it!
Amen.

63

Time to decide?

A listener to Jesus

As they were going along the road, someone said to him, 'I will follow you wherever you go.' And Jesus said to him, 'Foxes have holes, and birds of the air have nests; but the Son of Man has nowhere to lay his head.' To another he said, 'Follow me.' But he said, 'Lord, first let me go and bury my father.' But Jesus said to him, 'Let the dead bury their own dead; but as for you, go and proclaim the kingdom of God.' Another said, 'I will follow you, Lord; but let me first say farewell to those at my home.'

Luke 9:57–61

Meditation

Time to decide?
Come off it, what's the rush?
There's ages yet,
no hurry.
I want to live a little first,
let my hair down and enjoy myself.
You're only young once, after all –
time for the serious stuff later.

Time to decide?
Not yet, Lord –
tomorrow will do.
I'm busy right now,
no time to stop –
come back another day.
You understand, don't you?
It's not that I don't want to listen,
but there's the house, the garden, the job, the family –
so much to do and so little time to do it –
I'll get round to you eventually, I promise.

Time to decide?
I'm frightened, Lord –
scared of what you might ask,
what committing myself might involve.
I don't like to say no,
but I'm terrified of saying yes,
so give me a little longer,
just a few more days.
Please!

Time to decide?
Do I have to?
I'm happy with the way things are,
quite content to plod along –
why go upsetting the applecart?
Let's leave it for now, shall we? –
wait until the moment's right.
You don't mind, do you?

Time to decide?
Fair enough, Lord, I'm ready.
What was that?
Too late!
The decision made.
I don't understand what you mean.
Lord, I'm listening,
I'm ready!
Lord?

Prayer

Living God,
you do not force us to decide;
instead, you invite our response.
You do not dictate what we should do;
rather you want us to make up our own minds.
You are always there,
calling, coaxing, guiding, prompting,
but ultimately you leave decisions up to us.
Save us from running away from that challenge,
from putting off until tomorrow what we know should be tackled today,

and save us too from evading your call,
afraid of what it may involve.
Help us to listen for your voice and seek your will,
and, having done that as best we can,
give us the wisdom and courage we need to decide wisely.
Amen.

64

It seemed like a good idea at the time, Lord

A listener to Jesus

Jesus said to him, 'No one who puts a hand to the plough and looks back is fit for the kingdom of God.'

Luke 9:62

Meditation

It seemed a good idea at the time, Lord;
not just the right thing to do, but the only thing.
You called, and I responded,
freely, thankfully, gladly,
the joy of your love flooding my soul,
the promise of new life stretching out gloriously before me.
I'd made my decision
and I was happy to have done so,
confident of the way ahead.
Only then the doubts started,
not about you, but me,
my ability to honour the promise I'd made.
It wasn't that my love changed, don't think that;
simply that I began to understand what commitment involves.
Your call to love and go on loving,
give and go on giving;
to turn the other cheek,
forgive my enemies,
walk the extra mile –
I hadn't bargained on those,
and, together, they've made me realise that taking a decision is one thing,
living up to it quite another.
I'm scared, Lord,
afraid of letting you down,
of my faith proving to be all show and no substance.

I want to follow, you know that –
but I'm not sure I have what it takes to see it through.
Oh Lord, what have I done?
Where am I going?
You helped me decide;
now help me live with my decision!

Prayer

Lord Jesus Christ,
we have responded to your love
and committed ourselves to your service,
but we find it difficult to follow as we would wish,
hard to live up to the faith we profess.
You bring us joy and fulfilment,
but also a disturbing challenge,
calling us to a way of life that can be so demanding
we are left wondering quite what we've taken on.
Walk with us on our journey,
and help us to finish what we've started.
Amen.

65

'Who the devil do you think you are?'

Nicodemus

The Jews answered him, 'Are we not right in saying that you are a Samaritan and have a demon?' Jesus answered, 'I do not have a demon; but I honour my Father, and you dishonour me. Yet I do not seek my own glory; there is one who seeks it and he is the judge. Very truly, I tell you, whoever keeps my word will never see death.' The Jews said to him, 'Now we know that you have a demon. Abraham died, and so did the prophets; yet you say, "Whoever keeps my word will never taste death." Are you greater than our father Abraham, who died? The prophets also died. Who do you claim to be?' Jesus said to them, 'Very truly, I tell you, before Abraham was, I am.' So they picked up stones to throw at him, but Jesus hid himself and went out of the temple.

John 8:48–53, 58, 59

Meditation

'Who the devil do you think you are?'
That's what they were saying –
couched in different terms, admittedly,
put a little more politely,
but that's what they wanted to know.
'What gives you the right to come marching in here
as if you own the place?
Who gives you the authority to tell us what to do?'
And I knew what they were thinking beneath their pious expressions:
'What a nerve!
A jumped-up nobody from Galilee trespassing on our special territory.'
They were the experts, not *him*!
They were the ones who'd studied the Scriptures,
who knew the Law back to front,
who understood what God required!
It never occurred to them they could be wrong.
The possibility that all their religious zeal might be some empty facade
didn't even enter their heads.
I know, believe me, for I was the same once,

utterly convinced of my own righteousness until I heard Jesus for myself.
Then I had to see him again, talk to him face to face.
Don't ask me why – it was madness, foolhardy,
and if they ever find out they'll probably kill me, just as they killed him.
But suddenly I knew he offered more to life than I'd begun to realise,
and I had to find it for myself.
'Unless you are born again,' he told me,
you cannot see the kingdom of God.'
It seemed like nonsense at the time, and I went away disappointed,
back into the darkness.
But I'm beginning to understand now.
You see, I watched him after that,
as he taught,
as he healed,
as he suffered,
as he died . . .
and he did it all with such quiet dignity.
Yet my fellow Pharisees couldn't see it,
instead hounding him to the last –
spitting at him,
hitting him,
cursing him as he hung on that cross.
He said he was the Son of God, and I believe him.
He said he spoke for the Father, and I believe him.
He said he would rise again, and, call me a fool,
but I'm beginning to believe that too!
For I really feel that he's given me new life,
new beginnings,
here and now!

Prayer

Loving God,
you know us better than we know ourselves,
you search our hearts, minds and souls,
seeing us as we really are and confronting us with our true selves.
Forgive us that all too often we shy away from anything
that contradicts the image we have of ourselves;
that we find it hard to be honest,
closing our ears to truths we would rather not hear;
that we prefer those who soothe and flatter our egos

to those who challenge and disturb.
Give us true humility,
so that we may be ready to examine ourselves,
to ask searching questions,
and to change where necessary.
Amen.

Faith and works

66

I thought I'd heard wrongly

Amos

Alas for you who desire the day of the Lord! Why do you want the day of the Lord? It is darkness, not light; as if someone fled from a lion, and was met by a bear; or went into the house and rested a hand against the wall, and was bitten by a snake. Is not the day of the Lord darkness, not light, and gloom with no brightness in it? I hate, I despise your festivals, and I take no delight in your solemn assemblies. Even though you offer me your burnt offerings and grain offerings, I will not accept them; and the offerings of well-being of your fatted animals I will not look upon. Take away from me the noise of your songs; I will not listen to the melody of your harps. But let justice roll down like waters, and righteousness like an ever-flowing stream.

Amos 5:18–24

Meditation

I thought I'd heard wrongly,
my wires crossed somewhere,
for the message was scandalous,
too shocking even to contemplate, let alone proclaim.
Their sacrifices, meaningless?
Worship, empty?
Songs, noise?
Offerings, worthless?
It seemed little short of blasphemy,
a contradiction of everything I'd been taught since childhood,
and for a moment my world was thrown into confusion.
Yet there was no getting away from it:
that's what God was saying, loud and clear.
I struggled to take it in, you can imagine,
wondering what on earth it could all mean
and whether I could dare speak it.
All right, so maybe they weren't Judeans,
but then we can't all have everything, can we!
They were God's people, nonetheless,

a devout nation just as we were,
on the surface anyway –
scrupulous in outward piety,
meticulous in their attention to the Law,
the sort of people you'd find it hard to find fault with,
upright, decent, respectable,
pillars of the local community.
So what was the problem?
How could God condemn them?
Only then I stopped,
and looked not at their faith but at their lives,
at their witness rather than worship,
and suddenly I saw it, clear as day.
It was all show –
their zeal and piety an empty facade belying a hollow interior.
They praised God but served self,
preached justice but practised corruption,
their words saying one thing, their deeds another.
And the tragedy is they couldn't see it,
eyes blinded by the trappings of religion,
outward observance everything,
substance replaced by shadow.
Those have their place, don't get me wrong,
but only as a means to an end, never an end in themselves.
Forget that and there is nothing so sad and no one so lost;
for while you may think you have everything,
the reality is this:
you have nothing at all.

Prayer

Lord,
it's easy to go to church,
hard to reach out to the world;
easy to say our prayers,
hard to act upon them;
easy to offer our money,
hard to give you our lives;
easy to sing your praises,
hard to live to your glory.
Forgive us for so often taking the easy way;

the way of outward show rather than inner faith.
Move within us, so that the words of our lips
may show themselves in the thoughts of our hearts,
and the claims of our faith
be proven through the sincerity of our service.
Amen.

67

I hate to say it, but he was right

A Pharisee

'Beware of practising your piety before others in order to be seen by them; for then you have no reward from your Father in heaven.'

Matthew 6:1

Meditation

I hate to say it, but he was right,
his analysis of true worship and sacrifice spot on.
I'd fasted often and given generously,
even going short on occasions myself,
but commendable though it all seemed,
dedicated,
devout,
it was chiefly about me,
for my benefit as much as anyone's.
I'd *intended* to serve God,
and for a time thought I had,
but though I didn't exactly trumpet it,
I made quite sure others knew of my zeal in charity,
constancy in devotion,
and steadfastness in self-denial.
And there was more, besides,
for even my *unseen* acts of devotion were tarnished,
offered simply to bask in the glow of having done my bit,
or in the expectation of material reward.
Hearing Jesus, however, brought home to me that piety is not enough,
for God looks beneath the surface into the heart and mind,
assessing not only what we do but also why we do it.
the thought as well as the action,
and by that yardstick, I fear, I was measured and found wanting.
'So what now?' I hear you ask.
Will I still fast,
still deny myself,

still give to others?
Well yes, I certainly intend to,
but out of *love* this time,
joy instead of duty,
and as to where and when,
let alone how much or what,
don't ask me that,
or at least don't expect an answer if you do,
for I've learnt that some things are between me and him,
and are far best staying that way.

Prayer

Gracious God,
give us a heart devoted to you,
a mind focused on you,
a will committed to you,
a life dedicated to your service.
May our faith, service and witness never be a matter of routine,
offered out of a sense of duty or compulsion,
still less an empty going through the motions.
Above all,
save us from self-serving religion –
from a pseudo-discipleship aimed at salving our conscience,
earning rewards,
seeking our own ends
or bolstering our ego.
Teach us to love you for who and what you are,
seeking your will and walking your way for the sheer joy of doing so.
Amen.

68

Are we called to a faith that doesn't show?

Matthew

'And whenever you fast, do not look dismal, like the hypocrites, for they disfigure their faces so as to show others that they are fasting. Truly I tell you, they have received their reward. But when you fast, put oil on your head and wash your face, so that your fasting may be seen not by others but by your Father who is in secret; and your Father who sees in secret will reward you.'

Matthew 6:16–18

Meditation

Are we called to a faith that doesn't show,
a commitment none can see?
It sounds like it, doesn't it?
Yet he'd spoken, just moments earlier, of letting our light shine,
our good works speaking to others of God.
It's no incognito discipleship we're called to,
a faith ashamed to own its name,
but neither is it a self-serving discipleship,
speaking more of *us* than *him*.
And, believe me, that can happen,
more easily than you might think.
Those hypocrites he spoke of . . .
do you think they set out to parade their virtue?
They may do now,
but they were probably as sincere as any initially,
their prayers, almsgiving and fasting a sign of true devotion . . .
only for outward show, over the years, to replace inner substance.
Our relationships can grow stale,
even when it comes to God,
what once was natural as breathing becoming artificial,
forced,
put on for appearance only.

That's what Jesus was warning against –
faith that's become a facade,
more about being seen to look the part than anything real underneath.
Don't think about your good works,
still less display them,
or they'll be good no longer,
simply a means to an end.
Keep them between yourself and God,
a spontaneous loving response,
and then, truly, you'll give glory to him.

Prayer

Keep our faith real, Lord,
fresh and alive.
Save it from ever becoming a matter of habit or duty,
a going though the motions masking a lack of substance beneath.
Nurture and nourish our relationship with you,
so that our love always remains as natural, deep and sincere
as the day on which it first was born.
Amen.

69

Salt

A Galilean fisherman

'You are the salt of the earth; but if salt has lost its taste, how can its saltiness be restored? It is no longer good for anything, but is thrown out and trampled underfoot.'

Matthew 5:13

Meditation

Salt.
You can't get much more ordinary than that, can you?
We've got masses of the stuff,
enough in the Dead Sea alone, I shouldn't wonder,
to supply all the world's needs,
So when Jesus turned to us the other day and told us,
'You are the salt of the earth',
you can appreciate why I scarcely batted an eyelid –
it was hardly the highest accolade he could have given.
At least, that's what I thought then;
only *now* I'm having second thoughts,
for it's struck me since just how much we use salt for:
preserving,
purifying,
seasoning,
even healing wounds on the odd occasion –
such remarkable properties for so commonplace a substance.
It's one of those things we take for granted . . .
until we haven't got it . . .
and then, suddenly, we realise how much it's needed,
how vital is its role.
Is that what Jesus was saying to us:
that our role likewise is to preserve and purify,
to enhance the quality of people's lives,
to help heal this bleeding, broken world of ours –
not in any pretentious way,

blowing our own trumpet or parading our virtues.
but quietly,
without fuss,
in a way that's barely noticed yet indispensable nonetheless?
I think it is,
for isn't that precisely what he showed in his living for others,
his way of unassuming service,
gently yet irrevocably transforming the world.
It doesn't sound much: 'salt of the earth',
but it's actually the highest of compliments
and most awesome of challenges,
for it speaks of making a lasting difference to people's lives
and changing them for the better.
You can't get much more special than that, can you!

Prayer

Lord Jesus Christ,
thank you for the difference you have made to our lives
and those of so many people like us.
Thank you for the difference you have made to our world,
transforming innumerable situations across the centuries.
You call us, in turn, to make a difference –
to help bring joy, hope, help and healing to those who are hurting –
all who have lost their sense of purpose or faith in the future.
Forgive us for so often failing to honour that calling,
our discipleship making such a feeble impact on those around us.
Help us to be salt of the earth,
fit for use in your service.
Amen.

70

Had he made a mistake?

A listener to the Sermon on the Mount

'You are the light of the world. A city built on a hill cannot be hidden. No one, after lighting a lamp puts it under the bushel basket, but on the lampstand, and it gives light to all in the house. In the same way, let your light shine before others, so that they may see your good works and give glory to your Father in heaven.'

Matthew 5:14–16

Meditation

Had he made a mistake?
I thought he must have, at first.
'*You* are the light of the world'?
It had to be wrong, surely?
That was *him* wasn't it, not *us* –
he the one who brings light to those walking in darkness?
At least that's what I'd always believed:
that one day God would send a Messiah
whose glory would shine like a beacon in the world,
all nations drawn by his radiance
and nothing able to overshadow the brightness of his coming.
So what was *this* all about,
turning the tables on us
so that suddenly *we* were the ones called to be light,
we those with the responsibility of scattering the darkness?
It was the last thing I expected,
and the last thing I'd bargained on,
for I knew that, on my own, I could scarcely raise a flicker,
let alone a light bright enough to bring glory to God.
If it was down to *my* efforts,
my faith,
then there'd be no hope for anyone.
And, of course, he knew that full well.
It's *his* grace that floods our souls,

his love that fills our hearts,
his light that shines in our lives,
and without that we can do nothing.
But that doesn't mean we can simply sit back and let it happen,
for alongside what he has done for *us*
faith is about what we can do for *him*!
It involves giving as well as receiving,
serving as well as being served,
and we need to do that not simply when the mood takes us,
but every day,
every moment,
that call at the very heart of discipleship –
the essence of faith.
The light of the world –
yes, it means *you* as well as him,
for though ultimately *he* is the true light,
the one who illuminates the way for all,
he needs *your* love,
your deeds,
your compassion,
your faith translated into action
if the darkness is not to close in and his light be obscured.
'Let your light shine before others,
so that they may see your good works
and give glory to your Father in heaven.'

Prayer

Lord Jesus Christ,
it *does* sound stupid,
hiding a lamp under a bushel basket,
but you know that we do it all the time.
Instead of sharing what you have done for us,
we keep it to ourselves.
Instead of looking to the interests of others,
we focus on our own.
Instead of reaching out to those in need,
we shut our minds to their plight.
Time and again our words say one thing
and our lives another.
Forgive us our failure,

our neglect of our calling
and our dereliction of duty.
Help us to recognise that as a flame starved of oxygen will die,
so our light will finally be extinguished unless we share it with others.
Fill our hearts once more with the joy of your presence
and the knowledge of all you have done for us,
so that we may shine like beacons in the world,
and bring glory to our Father in heaven.
Amen.

71

It's a great picture, isn't it!

A listener to the Sermon on the Mount

'Everyone who hears these words of mine and acts on them will be like a wise man who built his house on rock. The rain fell, the floods came, and the winds blew and beat on that house, but it did not fall, because it had been founded on rock. And everyone who hears these words of mine and does not act on them will be like a foolish man who built his house on sand. The rain fell, and the floods came, and the winds blew and beat against that house, and it fell – and great was its fall!'

Matthew 7:24–27

Meditation

It's a great picture, isn't it –
a wonderful, almost ridiculous, contrast!
The wise man building his house on sure foundations
and the fool building his on the sand.
Could anyone be so stupid?
You wouldn't have thought so, would you?
And I was confident of one thing:
you wouldn't catch me making such a mistake,
not the slightest danger of that at all.
No, I understood that there's more to life than meets the eye;
more than money or material possessions, status or success,
for none of those are certain when the going gets hard
and the storms break over you.
I knew there had to be something else,
and in Jesus I thought I'd found it.
As I listened to his teaching and marvelled at his ministry,
as I saw for myself lives transformed,
broken, battered individuals healed, renewed, forgiven,
I decided that here was what life is all about,
and I rejoiced in his message of love and forgiveness.
I drank in his every word,
determined to make the blessings he spoke of mine,

confident of experiencing the joys of his kingdom.
Only then it came, just as he'd warned it would do –
the rain fell,
the floods rose,
the wind blew and beat against me –
and, with a sickening crash, I fell.
That's right, you heard me,
I fell!
Why?
Because I thought I'd obeyed, and I hadn't,
I thought I'd been wise, and I'd been a fool,
I thought I'd listened, and I'd barely heard,
ignoring the one thing that really mattered.
'Everyone,' he said, 'who hears these words of mine
and acts upon them
will be like a wise man who built his house on rock.'
I'd done the first but not the second,
the faith I professed being all words and no actions,
and now, when the moment came, I was found wanting,
life crumbling into the sand after all.
I'd come close, yet not close enough,
recognising that Jesus was the way, the truth and the life,
but accepting it only with my head,
not my heart.
Don't make my mistake.
Don't sit back believing you've done all that needs doing,
or, like me, you may be in for an unwelcome surprise.
It's not hearing his words that matters,
not even accepting they are true;
it's whether they make a difference to who you are,
whether you hear and act upon them
such that they change the way you live.

Prayer

Lord Jesus Christ,
we are good at talking,
poor when it comes to putting our words into practice.
We are happy to listen,
reluctant to act on what we have heard.
We are quick to make promises,

slow to honour them.
All too often our good intentions are not translated into reality,
our lives becoming a saga of what could and should have been.
We mean to respond to your call,
but we keep putting off a final decision.
Even when we do finally commit ourselves,
we are so easily led astray,
other interests, demands and attractions undermining our resolve.
Forgive us, despite your guidance,
for building our lives on sand rather than rock.
Open our ears,
so that we may not only hear but also act upon your word.
Amen.

72

I was enjoying the story at first

A Pharisee

Then he began to speak to them in parables. 'A man planted a vineyard, put a fence around it, dug a pit for the wine press, and built a watch-tower; then he leased it to tenants and went to another country. When the season came, he sent a slave to the tenants to collect from them his shares of the produce of the vineyard. But they seized him, and beat him, and sent him away empty-handed. And again he sent another slave to them; this one they beat over the head and insulted. Then he sent another, and that one they killed. And so it was with many others; some they beat, and others they killed. He had still one other, a beloved son. Finally he sent him to them, saying, "They will respect my son." But those tenants said to one another, "This is the heir; come, let us kill him, and the inheritance will be ours." So they seized him, killed him, and threw him out of the vineyard. What then will the owner of the vineyard do? He will come and destroy the tenants and give the vineyard to others. Have you not read this scripture: "The stone that the builders rejected has become the corner-stone; this was the Lord's doing, and it is amazing in our eyes"?' When they realised that he had told this parable against them, they wanted to arrest him, but they feared the crowd. So they left him and went away.

Mark 12:1–12

Meditation

I was enjoying the story at first –
a fascinating little tale of corruption and intrigue –
until, that is, I realised it was targeted at me and my fellow Pharisees.
What a nerve!
Do you understand what he was saying?
That *we* were the ones who, across the years, had obstructed God's will,
frustrated his purpose,
opposed his servants.
The very idea!
Preposterous, isn't it?
If anyone has been faithful, it's us,
our one aim and concern having been to discern God's guidance

and bring his kingdom closer.
So why the lecture?
Well, it wasn't hard to work that one out.
He was peeved, wasn't he? –
piqued by our refusal to swallow his fantastic claims
the way some had done,
and this was his way of getting back at us,
of venting his pent-up frustrations.
You'd have thought he might have learnt his lesson by then,
for we'd made no secret of our feelings,
our determination to bring him to justice.
But had he?
Not a bit of it,
for in that same ridiculous parable he was at it again,
spouting about the father sending his son,
the stone that the builders rejected becoming the chief cornerstone,
and we all know who he meant by that!
It was blasphemy, nothing less,
and though we could forgive him his attack upon us,
we could never accept this presumption against God,
this setting himself up as his gift to humankind.
No, in one thing at least he was right:
that final visitor to the vineyard will come to a sticky end;
not as soon as we'd like to see it –
the crowd won't stand for that –
but one day his time will come,
Jesus held up at last as a spectacle for all to see.
We don't like being heavy-handed, despite what he says,
but this man deserves death and he's going to get it;
and then we'll see, won't we, who's right and who's wrong?
Then we can judge, one way or the other,
just what is the Lord's doing!

Prayer

Lord Jesus Christ,
it never enters our heads that, far from serving you,
we might be obstructing your purpose,
that instead of living as your people,
we are frustrating your will,
our faithlessness actually inhibiting the growth of your kingdom.
We would never be false to you knowingly,
yet it can happen nonetheless,
our eyes blind to our faults,
our minds closed to all opinions other than our own.
Like the Pharisees of old, we can act in all sincerity,
convinced that *we* are being true to your cause
and that it is *others* who are out of step,
when the reality is precisely the opposite,
our preconceptions and prejudices,
our narrow vision and intolerant attitudes
serving to deny and undermine the very faith we proclaim.
Save us from making that mistake.
Challenge us when our faith grows stale,
open our eyes should our horizons become clouded
and restore us to your way when we go astray.
Remind us always that the truth lies in you and not ourselves,
and so help us to work with rather than against you,
for the growth of your kingdom,
through the renewing power of your Holy Spirit.
Amen.

73

I had no time for religion

A modern-day Christian

'What do you think? A man had two sons; he went to the first and said, "Son, go and work in the vineyard today." He answered, "I will not"; but later he changed his mind and went. The father went to the second and said the same; and he answered, "I go, sir"; but he did not go. Which of the two did the will of his father?' They said, 'The first.' Jesus said to them, 'Truly I tell you, the tax-collectors and the prostitutes are going into the kingdom of God ahead of you. For John came to you in the way of righteousness and you did not believe him, but the tax-collectors and the prostitutes believe him; and even after you saw it, you did not change your minds and believe him.'

Matthew 21:28–32

Meditation

I had no time for religion,
no interest in it at all.
Superstitious nonsense, that's what I thought.
And as for those who professed to follow it,
well, in my experience, they were a bunch of hypocrites,
no better than the rest of us, for all their airs and graces –
sanctimonious,
pious,
patronising.
I didn't want to know about it, thank you very much.
All right, so I wasn't perfect, not by a long way,
but at least I was genuine;
what you saw was what you got.
It wasn't only that, though;
I'd seen what religion can do to you –
the hang-ups it can cause,
the disputes,
intolerance,
sense of dependence –

all the opposite of what it's meant to be about.
Why get involved in that?
It was another world,
and I wanted no dealings with it,
my mind made up,
the decision final.
And then I encountered Jesus
and it all changed,
for here was someone different from anyone I'd ever met before –
nothing smug or pious about him,
not a trace of hypocrisy at all,
but a man who radiated sincerity,
whose life testified as words never could to the truth he proclaimed –
and I knew at once that he was someone special,
someone who accepted me as I was, with no strings attached.
So, after all those years of saying no, I finally said yes,
stunned yet ecstatic that anyone would offer me a second chance.
But shall I tell you something strange?
Though some welcomed me, most didn't.
Those same religious people from whom I'd expected a warm embrace,
looked away askance,
tight-lipped,
disapproving,
as patronising and sanctimonious as they'd ever been.
Their words said one thing,
their eyes another,
for all their talk of acceptance
the door to their hearts being firmly barred,
and I couldn't help but ask:
was it the same faith we shared,
or had one of us got it wrong?
We talked of faith,
and each believed we'd responded,
each certain we'd given our 'Yes' to God,
but something, somewhere didn't add up.
Can you explain it?

Prayer

Lord Jesus Christ,
we fool ourselves into believing
that the only thing involved in following you is confessing you as Lord;
as though one moment of decision,
one good intention,
is all that it takes.
Yet you tell us that many will cry to you, 'Lord, Lord',
and you will say to them that you never knew them.
Throughout your ministry,
you spoke not so much of a moment's conversion
as of a lifetime's service,
following you wherever you might lead.
Save us from imagining that we have done all that is necessary;
that a single declaration of faith has secured our eternal salvation.
Help us to understand that we are pilgrims on a journey
that has only just begun,
and give us strength to walk faithfully the course set before us,
as true to our calling tomorrow and the next day as we are today.
Amen.

74

They'll not thank me for saying this

The Apostle James

What good is it, my brothers and sisters, if you say you have faith but do not have works? Can faith save you? If a brother or sister is naked and lacks daily food, and one of you says to them, 'Go in peace; keep warm and eat your fill', and yet you do not supply their bodily needs, what is the good of that? So faith by itself, if it has no works, is dead. But someone will say, 'You have faith and I have works.' For just as the body without the spirit is dead, so faith without works is also dead.

James 2:14–17, 26

Meditation

They'll not thank me for saying this,
I can tell you that now,
but I'm going to say it anyway, whether they like it or not,
for it's too important a matter to keep quiet.
This business of faith and works,
we've made it all too easy,
too neat,
too comfortable,
so concerned with one truth that we've lost sight of another,
equally vital,
equally part of our response to Christ.
No, I'm not saying go back to the old way where works were everything,
where salvation was something to be earned –
I know what that's like,
struggling to obey the Law
in the vain hope we may deserve God's blessing,
and I can tell you from bitter experience that it's hopeless,
a road to nowhere.
But to veer in the opposite direction,
as though it must be all or nothing,
faith *or* works –
is that really any better?

Not in my book it isn't,
for what kind of faith is it that doesn't prove itself in action?
The proof of the pudding's in the eating, isn't that what they say?
And didn't Jesus himself teach much the same?
'Not everyone who says to me, "Lord, Lord",
will enter the kingdom of heaven,
but only the one who does the will of my Father in heaven.'
'For I was hungry and you gave me no food,
I was thirsty and you gave me nothing to drink,
I was a stranger and you did not welcome me,
naked and you did not give me clothing,
sick and in prison and you did not visit me.'
'Go away from me, you evil-doers,
I never knew you.'
It's disturbing, I know,
not the kind of thing we like to hear,
but it was Jesus who said it, not me,
so I reckon we'd do well to listen.
Of course we'll fail sometimes,
I realise that,
and of course we'll always finally be dependent on his grace –
without that we'd all be sunk, no hope for any of us –
but that doesn't mean our actions aren't important.
Think otherwise and you're in for a rude awakening.
We need faith *and* works,
for they're two sides of the same coin,
either of them without the other equally useless,
a pale imitation of the truth.
Ignore me if you want to,
it's up to you,
only remember this:
if what you practise is different from what you preach –
your words saying one thing but your deeds another –
then it's not just the world that will see through you,
it will be God as well.

Prayer

Lord,
to our shame our deeds rarely match up to our words.
We are full of fine-sounding ideals,
of lofty talk about serving others,
loving our neighbour,
taking the way of the cross,
but our actions put across a very different message.
In reality, little in our lives sets us apart from anyone else,
there being scant evidence of the faith we profess
or the Christ we claim to represent.
Forgive us, for until we learn to practise what we preach
few will take notice of the gospel.
Forgive us for making the good news seem like empty rhetoric
rather than the word of life,
and help us in the days ahead to show the truth of what we believe
through the things we do and the people we are.
Teach us not simply to proclaim Christ,
but to help make him real.
Amen.

Time and space for God

75

I had a shock today

The Psalmist

Lord, you have been our dwelling place in all the generations. Before the mountains were brought forth, or ever you had formed the earth and the world, from everlasting to everlasting you are God. You turn us back to dust, and say, 'Turn back you mortals.' For a thousand years in your sight are like yesterday when it is past, or like a watch in the night. You sweep them away; they are like a dream, like grass that is renewed in the morning; in the morning it flourishes and is renewed; in the evening it fades and withers. The days of our life are seventy years, or perhaps eighty, if we are strong; even then their span is only toil and trouble; they are soon gone, and we fly away.

Psalm 90:1–6, 10

Meditation

I had a shock today.
I caught sight of my reflection in a pool of water,
and I didn't recognise the man I saw there.
He looked old,
anxious,
weary,
the hair thinning and flecked with grey,
the forehead pitted with wrinkles,
the eyes heavy, full of trouble,
as though he bore the cares of the world on his shoulders,
and I thought, 'What a shame . . .
poor old fellow . . .
who's he?'
Only, of course, it was me,
those worn and jaded features reflecting the man I'd become,
and I was overwhelmed suddenly by an awareness of my mortality,
the fleeting nature of this brief span of ours,
here today and gone tomorrow.
Yes, I knew it before, in theory anyway,

but today it's hit home with a chilling intensity –
the stark realisation that life is rushing by and nothing can stop it;
that all our hopes and plans, toiling and striving,
finally come to nothing.
It's not a pleasant thought, is it?
Yet funnily enough I can live with that, just about,
for I know that though *I* may change, God does not,
his power, his purpose, being always the same.
It's not the fact of death that troubles me,
so much as the waste of life,
the way we fritter away the days God has given,
each one poisoned by our folly and sinfulness.
We all do it:
a thoughtless act here,
selfish deed there,
and before we know it the ripples are everywhere,
a multitude of lives caught in their wash –
so surprising a result from so little a splash.
There's no escape, not by ourselves –
we're all trapped in this vortex of destruction,
and only God can set us free.
We've no right to expect it –
his judgement is well deserved –
but if we ask in true humility,
if we acknowledge our faults and throw ourselves upon his grace,
he may yet hear our prayer and have mercy.
Remember that, my friend, while there's still time and life beckons,
for, though we can't change the future,
with God's help we can still shape the present.
Turn to him, and the years we are given may yet bring us joy,
our toil and trouble forgotten,
gladness to last us all our days.

Prayer

Living God,
we spend so much of our lives in ceaseless striving,
pursuing first this, then that.
We labour,
we fret,
we fight,

we struggle,
our thoughts too often focused on present gain
and immediate satisfaction.
Yet all the goals that consume us bring but a moment's pleasure,
each destined to fade away.
Teach us to set our hearts first on you,
and to discover the fulfilment you offer in both this life and the next.
Help us to live not just in the context of our brief earthly span,
but in the light of your eternal purpose
in which, by your grace, you invite us all to share.
Amen.

76

'The fear of the Lord is the beginning of wisdom'

Solomon

My child, do not forget my teaching, but let your heart keep my commandments; for length of days and years of life and abundant welfare they will give you. Do not let loyalty and faithfulness forsake you; bind them around your neck, write them on the tablet of your heart. So you will find favour and good repute in the sight of God and of people. Trust in the Lord with all your heart, and do not rely on your own insight. In all your ways acknowledge him, and he will make straight your paths. Do not be wise in your own eyes; fear the Lord, and turn away from evil. It will be a healing for your flesh and a refreshment for your body.

Proverbs 3:1–8

Meditation

'The fear of the Lord is the beginning of wisdom' –
that's what my mother told me when I was just a boy,
and I've remembered it ever since,
a rule of thumb that's never left me.
A bit of a cliché, perhaps,
the words in danger of tripping off the tongue
just that bit too easily,
but better that than for them never to stick at all.
And it can happen, believe me,
the lesson we thought we'd learnt today,
forgotten tomorrow,
the truth we thought we'd fathomed
returning unexpectedly to perplex us.
Don't think you're different, for you're not.
We can all lose sight of the things that matter,
every one of us.
Slowly but surely we start to drift,
now this way, now that,
drawn by hidden currents inexorably onwards

until the shore we started from is lost to view.
I've witnessed it all too often,
principles compromised,
scruples forgotten,
as, little by little, the truth is eroded,
worn down by the unrelenting tide
of a hostile and dismissive world.
Yet it needn't be like that,
not if you remember what really counts:
the word of the Lord,
the commandments he's given,
the witness of his servants.
Make time for those,
not just to read them but to make them part of you,
engraved on your heart,
inscribed in your soul,
and you will find the way to life,
a light to guide you every step you take,
wholeness in body, mind and spirit.
That's what my mother taught me, all those years ago,
and that's what I've set out to teach in turn,
to share something of the wisdom she shared with me.
Not her wisdom, you understand,
or mine,
but springing from the fear of the Lord,
sustained and nurtured by him.
Discover that,
take that lesson to heart,
and you will find treasure indeed,
riches beyond price.

Prayer

Gracious God,
you have spoken your word,
you offer us guidance,
yet all too often we go astray.
Despite our desire to serve you,
we are swayed by those around us,
our faith undermined,
our beliefs subtly influenced by pressures

we are barely even aware of.
Forgive the weakness of our commitment
and teach us to make time for you each day,
to study your word and to reflect on your goodness.
Draw near to us
and help us to draw near to you,
so that you may be more fully a part of us,
filling us in heart and mind and soul.
Amen.

77

I thought I knew him better than most

Isaiah

Seek the Lord while he may be found, call upon him while he is near; let the wicked forsake their way, and the unrighteous their thoughts; let them return to the Lord, that he may have mercy on them, and to our God, for he will abundantly pardon. For my thoughts are not your thoughts, nor are your ways my ways, says the Lord. For as the heavens are higher than the earth, so are my ways higher than your ways and my thoughts than your thoughts. For as the rain and the snow come down from heaven, and do not return there until they have fed and watered the earth, making it bring forth and sprout, giving seed to the sower and bread to the eater, so shall my word be that goes out from my mouth; it shall not return to me empty, but it shall accomplish that which I purpose, and succeed in the thing for which I sent it.

Isaiah 55:6–11

Meditation

I thought I knew him better than most,
that over the years I'd come to understand him
as few have even begun to.
And I suppose I had, to a point,
for I'd glimpsed the wonder of his presence,
heard the sound of his voice,
and, by his grace, declared his purpose and made known his love:
good news for all the world.
Impressed?
You shouldn't be –
for it was nothing,
just the merest glimmer of light,
a tiny window on to an indescribable world of mystery.
Oh it was special, don't get me wrong,
every moment of my ministry a privilege that I will always treasure,
shaping *my* life and that of countless others.
I spoke of love, and my heart thrilled within me,
leaping like a deer sensing streams of life-giving water.

I spoke of forgiveness,
a fresh start,
new beginnings for us all,
and my spirit sang for joy,
dancing in exultation.
I spoke of light shining in the darkness,
reaching out into the gloom,
reviving, renewing, restoring,
and my soul exulted.
Yes, it was magical, no question,
but I'd glimpsed just a fraction of the whole,
a speck of flotsam in the vast and unfathomable ocean that is God.
Whatever I'd seen, far more lay hidden;
whatever I'd grasped, far more was yet to be revealed;
whatever I thought I'd understood, far more remained out of reach,
too awesome even to contemplate;
for we were different,
he before all and over all,
sovereign over space and time,
and me? –
a fleeting breath,
passing shadow,
like the flower of the field, here today and gone tomorrow.
I thought I knew him, better than any,
and to be fair, I did,
my knowledge of him growing each day –
new insights,
new discoveries,
new wonders beyond imagining,
but I recognise now that, however far I've come,
there's further still to go,
more yet to learn –
for all my travelling,
the journey's only just begun!

Prayer

Sovereign God,
all too often we lose sight of your greatness,
settling instead for a picture of you we feel comfortable with.
We frustrate your will through the smallness of our vision.

We miss opportunities to serve you
through the narrowness of our horizons.
We deny ourselves your mercy
through the confines we place upon your grace.
Time and again we presume that your ways are *our* ways
and your thoughts *our* thoughts,
forgetting that you are beyond words or human understanding.
Forgive us,
and teach us never to underestimate the awesomeness of your being
or the extent of your love.
Amen.

78

He was right, wasn't he!

Nicodemus

Nicodemus said to him, 'How can anyone be born after having grown old? Can one enter a second time into the mother's womb and be born?' Jesus answered, 'Very truly, I tell you, no one can enter the kingdom of God without being born of water and Spirit. What is born of the flesh is flesh, and what is born of the Spirit is spirit. Do not be astonished that I said to you, "You must be born from above." The wind blows where it chooses, and you hear the sound of it, but you do not know where it comes from or where it goes. So it is with everyone who is born of the Spirit.' Nicodemus said to him, 'How can these things be?' Jesus answered him, 'Are you a teacher of Israel, and yet you do not understand these things?'

John 3:4–10

Meditation

He was right, wasn't he!
I, of all people, should have understood his words –
me, a respected Pharisee,
teacher of Israel,
acknowledged expert in matters of faith.
Yet, listening to Jesus, I was like a child,
struggling to make sense of what he said.
'How can this be?' I asked.
'What do you mean?'
And, believe me, I really wanted to know.
I was risking everything, remember, even *talking* to him –
that's why I went at night –
for I was consorting with the enemy,
with someone my colleagues deemed a blasphemer,
but there was something about the man that held me spellbound,
his life speaking uniquely of God,
cutting through the paraphernalia
with which we'd so earnestly surrounded him.
I wasn't just picking holes,

arguing for the sake of debate.
I was hungry to learn and understand.
And for all that his words sometimes shocked me,
I couldn't help feeling Jesus had the answers I was looking for,
the keys, if you like, to the kingdom.
So I asked,
and I pondered,
and I asked again,
before returning home with my mind in a whirl,
past certainties shaken,
new ideas warring with old.
I'm still as confused as ever in some ways,
for I can't explain all that stuff about new beginnings
and being born again,
but I'm certain of one thing:
that what matters is responding to Jesus, not having all the answers;
that if we give him both our faith and doubt
we'll receive back far more than we can ask or expect –
life unlike anything we've known before!

Prayer

Almighty God,
make us hungry to know you better –
to understand more of your purpose,
more of your love in Christ,
more of what you would have us do and be.
Give us enquiring minds,
eager to explore the mysteries of faith
and to grow in understanding.
But help us also to recognise the limitations of our knowledge –
the fact that some things are and always will be beyond us –
and grant us then the humility to live with questions,
trusting in what we know and leaving the rest with you.
Amen.

79

I felt sorry for Martha, I really did

Mary, sister of Martha and Lazarus

Now as they went on their way, he entered a certain village, where a woman named Martha welcomed him into her home. She had a sister named Mary, who sat at the Lord's feet and listened to what he was saying. But Martha was distracted by her many tasks; so she came to him and asked, 'Lord, do you not care that my sister has left me to do all the work by myself? Tell her then to help me.'

Luke 10:38–40

Meditation

I felt sorry for Martha, I really did;
she was doing her best after all.
Someone had to see to the hospitality,
make sure the dinner was all right,
wash up after us,
and, to be honest, I felt I wasn't pulling my weight.
I could see she was getting harassed
despite the smile she kept on her face.
She didn't say anything, but she didn't need to,
I could tell by the way she looked that she was angry.
And with good reason.
It was selfish of me,
unforgivable,
but I couldn't help myself.
Jesus was so fascinating,
so easy to listen to,
so genuine.
It was as though every word he spoke was for me,
answering the questions I'd never dared to ask,
meeting the needs I never even knew existed,
giving me the sense of purpose I had so longed to find.
How could I get up to wash dishes;
interrupt him to offer another drink?

It would have been sacrilege.
I knew I might never have another chance like that again,
and so, shame on me, I sat back and let Martha get on with it.
I wasn't surprised when she finally complained,
but I was by the answer Jesus gave her.
I expected him to back her up, give *me* a ticking off –
after all, fair's fair.
But instead he praised me
and rebuked her!
He spoke gently, of course,
almost tenderly,
yet it was a rebuke for all that.
I don't know how *she* felt
but I could have died of embarrassment.
It was my fault, you see –
me who effectively earned her that reprimand,
and I expected her to be furious afterwards;
I know *I* would have been.
Yet, funnily enough, she wasn't.
She was very quiet for a time,
thoughtful,
and then she told me not to look so guilty,
for Jesus had been right.
He'd made her face herself for the first time, so she said,
and she realised now she couldn't go on running for ever,
couldn't go on hoping being busy would disguise the emptiness inside.
She'd been made to stop and ask herself what life was all about,
and in Jesus she had begun to find the answers.
She's still the efficient hostess, of course,
always will be.
And me?
I'm just as ready to find an excuse for laziness given half the chance!
But we've changed, both of us,
grown closer,
become more at peace with ourselves,
because, through meeting Jesus,
we've each discovered what really counts,
the one thing we really need.

Prayer

Loving God,
we think we are so busy, so pressurised.
We rush around day after day with never a moment to spare.
Yet so often we forget the one thing we really need:
to make time and space in our lives to meet with you,
to hear your voice,
and to look at the world from your perspective.
Teach us to be still and to know you are God.
Amen.

80

Don't feel sorry for me

Martha

But the Lord answered her, 'Martha, Martha, you are worried and distracted by many things; there is need of only one thing. Mary has chosen the better part, which will not be taken away from her.'

Luke 10:41, 42

Meditation

Don't feel sorry for me,
as if I was harshly judged,
unfairly treated,
for I wasn't,
not in the slightest.
Yes, there were jobs to be done –
the meal to prepare for a start –
but Jesus was in no hurry,
and neither should I have been.
The daft thing is it was *me* who invited him round,
not Mary;
I the one initially who recognised a gap in our lives
that Jesus alone could fill.
But I allowed myself to get distracted,
led into a blind alley by tasks that,
though worthy enough in themselves,
finally counted for nothing.
Not that Jesus minded, even then.
He knew I meant well and would listen eventually.
It was my *complaints* that stirred a response:
my seeking to land Mary in it,
as though she were at fault and I virtuous,
when the true error was mine.
He rebuked me for that,
if you can call it a rebuke,
but his words were patient,

gentle,
explaining rather than condemning,
inviting me to pause and think again.
I'm learning to do that, slowly,
making time to stop and stare, relax and reflect,
and I've found true rest in doing so,
not just for the body but for the soul.
It doesn't come easy to me,
for I'm the fussing sort,
always on tenterhooks,
but Jesus taught me a vital lesson that day:
there's a difference between what *seems* to matter
and what *really does*.

Prayer

Teach us, Lord, that, however busy we are,
however frenetic our lifestyle,
we need time to ponder,
time for you.
Forgive us that that we relegate you to the margins of our lives,
believing we have more important things to do,
more pressing concerns to see to.
Remind us that you have the words of eternal life,
the answer to our inner hunger and true needs,
and so, in our list of daily priorities,
help us to put you *first*,
not *last*.
Amen.

81

I didn't like to ask again

The Apostle James

He said to them, 'Suppose one of you has a friend, and you go to him at midnight and say to him, "Friend, lend me three loaves of bread; for a friend of mine has arrived, and I have nothing to set before him." And he answers from within, "Do not bother me; the door has already been locked, and my children are with me in bed; I cannot get up and give you anything." I tell you, even though he will not get up and give him anything because he is his friend, at least because of his persistence he will get up and give whatever he needs. So, I say to you, Ask, and it will be given you; search, and you will find; knock, and the door will be opened for you. For everyone who asks receives, and everyone who searches finds, and for everyone who knocks, the door will be opened. Is there anyone among you who, if your child asks for a fish, will give a snake instead of a fish? Or if the child asks for an egg, will give a scorpion? If you then, who are evil, know how to give good gifts to your children, how much more will the heavenly Father give the Holy Spirit to those who ask him!'

Luke 11:5–13

Meditation

I didn't like to ask again,
for I'd come before God in prayer so many times before,
and I was afraid if I kept on he'd get fed up with me,
sick and tired of the same old refrain, day after day.
There's no denying it,
I'd been like a dog with a bone,
refusing to let go
until even *I* had become wearied by the whole business,
never mind what *he* must have felt.
Yet, for all my pleading, I was no further forward,
my prayers seeming to fall on deaf ears –
hardly a surprise, then, that I lost heart.
It was time to give it a rest,
for if God wanted to answer me
he'd surely have done so by now,

it stood to reason –
even *his* patience has some limits!
Only I couldn't have been more wrong,
not just about that but about everything,
as Jesus was to show me so simply yet so powerfully that day.
Which of you, he said, wouldn't grant a request
if pushed hard enough?
If someone made a sufficient nuisance of themselves,
how many of you wouldn't give in? –
with bad grace perhaps,
against your better judgement,
but eventually any inconvenience worth it for a bit of peace.
I thought he was saying the same about God –
that if even *we* finally acquiesce,
then he is bound to do the same –
and perhaps that was part of it,
in the sense that we must never give up in prayer,
never feel he hasn't heard or doesn't care.
But then Jesus continued:
'Ask, and it will be given you;
search, and you will find;
knock, and the door will be opened for you' –
and I realised he wasn't so much comparing as contrasting God with us,
reminding us that, though it may not seem like it,
he is always listening,
always ready to respond,
always looking to grant his blessings to us.
So I'm here again,
kneeling before God,
offering once more my old familiar prayer,
and suddenly the answer is becoming clear –
goodness knows why I didn't see it before.
I should have done,
and I will next time,
for I know now he doesn't grudgingly reply when we call –
our prayers an unwelcome irritation.
Rather, he delights to hear us,
and waits eagerly to shower his blessing on all who ask him.
Thanks be to God.

Prayer

Lord Jesus Christ,
we know that God hears our prayers,
that he is ready to answer when we call to him,
but we are still reluctant sometimes to ask for help,
for we are conscious of having asked for it so many times before.
We seek forgiveness for the same old mistakes.
We ask for help with the same old problems.
We look for guidance concerning the same old matters.
We intercede for the same old people.
Day after day,
week after week,
we bring the same list of requests,
so familiar that even *we* have grown tired of them.
We are afraid of exhausting his patience,
of becoming an irritation and a nuisance,
and we wonder whether we are asking for the wrong things
or whether perhaps God has given his answer,
only we have failed to hear.
Yet you tell us he is always ready to listen,
always wanting to bless us,
and that no matter how often we approach him,
he will make time to hear us and time to answer.
Teach us then to approach with confidence
and to bring all our needs in faith before him,
assured that he longs to meet our need
and that, in his own time and way, he *will* respond.
Amen.

82

There was so much I wanted to ask

Peter

Then Jesus told them a parable about their need to pray always and not to lose heart. He said, 'In a certain city there was a judge who neither feared God nor had respect for people. In that city there was a widow who kept coming to him and saying, "Grant me justice against my opponent." For a while he refused; but later he said to himself, "Though I have no fear of God and no respect for anyone, yet because this widow keeps bothering me, I will grant her justice, so that she may not wear me out by continually coming."' And the Lord said, 'Listen to what the unjust judge says. And will not God grant justice to his chosen ones who cry to him day and night? Will he delay long in helping them? I tell you, he will quickly grant justice to them. And yet, when the Son of Man comes, will he find faith on earth?'

Luke 18:1–8

Meditation of Peter

There was so much I wanted to ask,
so much I longed to bring before God in prayer,
yet, somehow, I just couldn't bring myself to do it.
Does that sound strange to you?
It should do,
though if you're anything like I was
you'll understand well enough.
You see, it was God we were talking about here,
the Creator of heaven and earth,
above and beyond all,
Alpha and Omega,
sovereign in his holiness –
who was I to dare approach such a one?
He had other matters to attend to,
other business of more pressing concern;
and, even if he found time,
what interest could he have in a miserable wretch like me –
stubborn,

wilful,
disobedient,
just about as far removed from him as it's possible to be?
So that was that,
my dealings with God, such as they were,
being carried out at arm's length,
with no suggestion of meaningful dialogue
or a personal relationship.
It took that outrageous parable of Jesus to teach me sense –
a contrast so ridiculous yet so obvious
that even I had to sit up and take notice.
For he was right, wasn't he?
Even the worst of us,
the most unfeeling, uncaring and unjust,
have our threshold,
a point at which, for the sake of peace if nothing else,
we hear someone out and respond to their plea.
And if that's true with us, then where does it leave God,
the one we call good,
gracious,
compassionate,
slow to anger and swift to bless,
full of justice and righteousness,
rich in mercy and abounding in steadfast love?
How can we say all that and still hold back,
still imagine he does anything else but delight in our prayers
and hunger to grant our requests?
I forget that sometimes, even now,
the old idea of God remote in splendour still rearing its ugly head,
but, when that happens, I think again of those words of Jesus,
I picture that judge cursing
as, reluctantly, he grants the woman's request,
and then I offer my prayer,
confidently,
joyfully,
without reserve,
knowing that the Father is there as always,
ready to listen,
to speak,
and to grant his blessing.

Prayer

Lord Jesus Christ,
the way, the truth and the life,
we thank you for revealing the nature of God to us,
for demonstrating so wonderfully his grace and goodness,
his unfailing love and constant involvement in our lives.
All too easily we picture him instead as stern and remote,
set apart in his holiness,
easily angered and swift to punish;
a God to approach with fear and trembling
rather than in joyful response.
But you remind us that his nature is always to have mercy,
that his care can never be exhausted,
that he delights in knowing us
and longs to shower us with his blessings.
You have shown us the Father,
and we praise you for it.
Amen.

83

I'm not sure what we were expecting

Andrew

He was praying in a certain place, and after he had finished, one of his disciples said to him, 'Lord, teach us to pray, as John taught his disciples.'

Luke 11:1

Meditation

I'm not sure what we were expecting,
but we wanted help,
for we found prayer as much of a struggle as anyone.
We did our best, yes,
but when it came to communing with God,
opening up before him and hearing his voice,
we were floundering,
all at sea.
Not Jesus, though.
For him prayer appeared to come naturally,
instinctive and spontaneous;
every moment –
not just those set apart for God –
were seemingly lived in dialogue with the Father,
as though the two were one.
What was his secret, we wanted to know?
What method should we follow,
techniques use,
aids employ?
But he offered none of those,
just a prayer of his own,
incredibly short and simple yet saying it all –
a reminder if ever there was one that, when we pray,
it's not the number of words that matters
but the attitude behind them:
our willingness to seek God's glory,
accept his will

and work for his kingdom here on earth;
to trust in his love and accept his forgiveness,
responding to others in turn.
Approach God with such thoughts in your heart,
speak and listen as best you can,
give time to him,
and though it may still not come easily,
you'll have learnt what it means to pray.

Prayer

Teach us, Lord,
instead of looking for secrets of prayer,
some special method or formula that will make it easy,
to look to *you*,
making time to study your word,
seek your presence
and nurture a meaningful daily relationship.
Help us honestly, regularly and simply
to express what lies on our heart,
and show us, in turn, what lies on yours.
Amen.

84

They came as such a relief, those words of his

Andrew

Then Jesus told them a parable about their need to pray always and not to lose heart. He said, 'In a certain city there was a judge who neither feared God nor had respect for people. In that city there was a widow who kept coming to him and saying, "Grant me justice against my opponent." For a while he refused; but later he said to himself, "Though I have no fear of God and no respect for anyone, yet because this widow keeps bothering me, I will grant her justice, so that she may not wear me out by continually coming."' And the Lord said, 'Listen to what the unjust judge says. And will not God grant justice to his chosen ones who cry to him day and night? Will he delay long in helping them?'

Luke 18:1–7

Meditation

They came as such a relief, those words of his,
for I'm as guilty as any,
tending to badger God in prayer,
refusing to take no for an answer.
I'd been wondering if that was wrong,
if God would get sick and tired of the same old refrain day after day,
perhaps even ignore me as a result,
so I'd resolved to give it a rest,
lest I test his patience too far.
Only I couldn't have been more wrong,
as Jesus brought home so clearly in that wonderful parable of his.
I thought at first he was likening God to some reprobate judge –
some cantankerous old so-and-so who, though reluctant to hear,
can finally be worn down if we persist long enough –
but that wasn't the point at all,
for Jesus wasn't so much comparing as *contrasting* God,
emphasising that the two couldn't be more different.
Though we may not realise it, he is *always* listening,

always looking to respond,
always eager to grant his blessing,
so if he seemingly fails to answer,
it's not because he doesn't want to,
still less that we've asked too often,
but because his reply is yet to come.
It may not be today,
or tomorrow,
or tomorrow after that,
but never be afraid to ask and ask again,
for if anyone delights to hear, and promises to answer,
it's surely *him*.

Prayer

Thank you, Lord, that though we struggle in prayer,
finding ourselves lost for words
or endlessly repeating ourselves,
always you listen,
never tired of hearing us.
Teach us, then, to persevere,
looking for your answer until it becomes clear –
not necessarily the response we hope for,
but always the reply we need.
Amen.

New beginnings

85

He was right, of course

Nicodemus

'No one sews a piece of unshrunk cloth on an old cloak; otherwise, the patch pulls away from it, the new from the old, and a worse tear is made. And no one puts new wine into old wineskins; otherwise, the wine will burst the skins, and the wine is lost, and so are the skins; but one puts new wine into fresh wineskins.'

Mark 2:21, 22

Meditation

He was right, of course,
it doesn't do to mix the old with the new;
try that and you risk losing both.
Only it's one thing applying that to wine or pieces of cloth,
quite another when it comes to faith,
the gulf between them and the implications involved
being world's apart.
Yet that's what he seemed to be suggesting
through that illustration of his:
a break with the past,
parting of the ways,
revolution in our thinking.
That took some getting used to,
for everything we held dear was rooted in history,
built up over the centuries,
a priceless tradition of which we were justly proud.
Little wonder that some took offence at his words.
How could we throw it all aside?
It was too much to ask.
Only, of course, he wasn't asking that at all,
in fact, in many ways, quite the opposite.
He left us in no doubt where he stood:
'Do not think I have come to abolish the Law or the prophets;
I have come not to abolish but to fulfil.

Truly I tell you,
until heaven and earth pass away,
not one letter,
not one stroke of a letter,
will pass from the Law until all is accomplished.'
You can't get much clearer than that, can you?
No, he wasn't destroying the Law
so much as reinterpreting it,
getting down to its true meaning;
and that meant us moving on in our understanding,
broadening our horizons,
recognising that the way of Christ cannot be tied down
to what has gone before.
The old has its place and always will have,
a lamp to our people across the centuries that still has power to guide,
but a new light has dawned,
a new beginning,
which inevitably means change;
not just in the trimmings of religion –
ritual, ceremony and observance –
but in every part of life,
body, mind and soul.
He calls us to put off the old self and put on the new,
to start afresh,
be born again,
for only then can we share in the wine he brings.
It's painful to let go, I know,
to put behind you what has become so familiar
that it is almost part of you,
and, believe me, I'm struggling with it as much as anyone,
but he's helped me to see that there's no other way,
no other option that will do,
for if we cling to the past,
not only will we lose sight of the present,
we will never embrace the future.

Prayer

Lord Jesus Christ,
we are not good at letting go of the past,
at recognising there are times when we need to move on in life
and take a step forward in faith if we are ever truly to grow.
We prefer the security of the familiar,
the comfort of that which does not stretch or challenge us too far,
and we are wary of the prospect of change,
afraid that it might ask more of us than we are willing to give.
We are not good at letting go of the old and putting on the new;
at turning away from our former way of life
and taking instead the way of the cross;
at trusting in your guidance
and walking in the power of your Spirit.
We are reluctant to abandon old habits,
fearful of being thought different,
unwilling to deny ourselves the pleasures of this world
for the promise of the world to come.
So we try to keep a foot in both camps,
to combine the old with the new.
We think we can balance the two,
but, of course, we can't,
the end result being to compromise both and embrace neither.
Help us to understand that, while the old has its place,
there are some areas in life where a complete break is needed,
a turning away from what *has been*
before we are ready to receive what *shall be*.
Lord Jesus Christ,
you want to work within us
to finish the new creation you have begun.
Give us courage to trust you completely,
so that you may truly refashion our lives.
Amen.

86

It didn't make sense

The man born blind

So for the second time they called the man who had been blind, and they said to him, 'Give glory to God! We know that this man is a sinner.' He answered, 'I do not know whether he is a sinner. One thing I do know, that though I was blind, now I see.' They said to him, 'What did he do to you? How did he open your eyes? . . . We know that God has spoken to Moses, but as for this man, we do not know where he comes from.' The man answered, 'Here is an astonishing thing! You do not know where he comes from, and yet he opened my eyes.'

John 9:24–26, 29, 30

Meditation

It didn't make sense,
for I'd been blind all my life,
yet now could see more clearly than anyone –
not just with my eyes
but with my soul.
He'd healed me, that man Jesus,
made me whole,
but those blinkered Pharisees wouldn't have it,
rejecting him instead as a sinner
and insinuating it was all some trick,
a sinister sleight of hand.
Not that I was surprised,
for they'd condemned me equally,
suggesting my condition was divinely ordained,
punishment for some unnamed crime,
but Jesus showed otherwise,
demonstrating that sorrow and suffering are not willed by God,
but part of the fabric of our broken world,
contrary to his design
and one day to be transformed.
For me that time had come,

the darkness lifted at the touch of his hand
and light flooding my life.
Yet those who should have understood seemed baffled,
unable to see the wood for the trees.
It's a mystery to me,
for he was so clearly sent from God,
not just working in his name but revealing his love,
yet somehow they couldn't see what was staring them in the face.
Wonderfully, amazingly, he opened my eyes,
but theirs, despite it all, stayed closed.

Prayer

Loving God,
hear our prayer for those whose minds are closed to you,
unable or unwilling to recognise your love.
Speak your word to all who cannot or will not hear –
those who angrily reject you
or who simply dismiss you as irrelevant to their lives.
And speak also to us,
for though we may have responded to you in faith
we are still guilty at times of shutting you out,
selective in what we accept and what we prefer not to.
Break through the walls of hostility, doubt, arrogance and apathy,
and reveal your grace and goodness in Christ.
Amen.

87

It was so weird

Lazarus

Then Jesus, again greatly disturbed, came to the tomb. It was a cave, and a stone was lying against it. Jesus said, 'Take away the stone.' Martha, the sister of the dead man, said to him, 'Lord, already there is a stench because he has been dead four days.' Jesus said to her, 'Did I not tell you that if you believed, you would see the glory of God?' So they took away the stone. And Jesus looked upward and said, 'Father, I thank you for having heard me. I knew that you always hear me, but I have said this for the sake of the crowd standing here, so that they may believe that you sent me.' When he had said this, he cried with a loud voice, 'Lazarus, come out!' The dead man came out, his hands and feet bound with strips of cloth, and his face wrapped in a cloth. Jesus said to them, 'Unbind him, and let him go.'

John 11:38–44

Meditation

It was so weird,
so unreal.
At least that's how it felt.
And yet it happened!
I'd breathed my last, no question about that.
After those long dark days of sickness,
the pain growing
the strength failing;
after those final terrible hours,
sweat pouring down my face,
lungs gasping for air;
at last came peace,
darkness closing about me,
suddenly welcome though it had long been feared.
An end to the struggle,
the battle nearly over.
For a moment I was a child again, comforted by my mother's embrace,
a youth running wild as the wind,

a man setting out afresh on life's great adventure,
a father, taking my child into my arms.
And then rest.
The light went out,
the flame extinguished,
the game completed.
Only it wasn't,
for suddenly a voice summoned me back to the fray,
sunshine burst into the tomb,
and consciousness returned.
No wonder they gasped,
swooned,
wept for joy,
for I who had been taken from them,
who had been dead,
was alive!
And yes, I thanked Jesus, of course I did,
once the confusion had cleared anyway,
but it took a while, I can tell you.
And even now just once in a while
I wonder if he really did me any favours,
for I know that one day I must face it all over again.
Yet it will be different then,
very different,
not just because I've been there before and know there's nothing to fear,
but because he has shown me that death is not so much the end
as the beginning.
That's why he raised me from the tomb.
Not just to restore life or defer death,
but to point to a new birth,
a resurrection that only he can bring.
He came back too, you know,
back from beyond the grave.
Three days in his tomb,
long enough for decay to take hold,
but he appeared to Mary,
to Peter,
to the apostles,
to us all.
That's how we know that,
even though we die,

one day we shall live,
just as he lives now!

Prayer

Lord Jesus Christ,
you came to bring us life in all its fullness;
to offer hope beyond the grave.
Teach us that death is not the end, but a new beginning –
the gateway to life everlasting.
And may that confidence shape our attitude not only towards death
but towards life also.
May we live each day in the context of eternity
rather than simply of the here and now,
knowing there is nothing in heaven or earth
that will ever finally be able to separate us from your love.
Amen.

88

He called me out of the tomb

Lazarus

He cried with a loud voice, 'Lazarus, come out!' The dead man came out, his hands and feet bound with strips of cloth, and his face wrapped in a cloth. Jesus said to them, 'Unbind him, and let him go.'

John 11:43a, 44

Meditation

He called me out of the tomb,
his words somehow reaching into the darkness
and restoring life.
One moment, oblivion –
and the next I was up on my feet,
shuffling out of the tomb.
One moment, trussed up like a chicken,
mummified before my time,
and the next scratching my head in bewilderment,
baffled by the look on their faces.
They thought me a ghost,
gazing in astonishment and reaching out in disbelief.
I'd been dead,
and was alive again,
really alive –
not just existing as I'd done previously,
but enthused with a joy such as I'd never known before,
set free not just from my grave clothes
but from everything that had held me captive,
denying and destroying life.
I'll die eventually, of course,
just like anyone else,
but he summoned me from the grave,
defeating the power of death,
and I know now that, in the fullness of time,
he's able to do the same again and more besides,

not just for me
but for all.

Prayer

Eternal God,
thank you for the hope you give us –
a hope that will not disappoint.
Thank you for the knowledge that
though this life must come to an end –
its conclusion bringing with it the trauma of bereavement,
the anguish of losing loved ones,
the bleak awareness of our own mortality –
we are able, finally, to face death
not with despair, fear or resignation,
but in quiet confidence
assured that it is a stepping stone to new beginnings,
the start of a fresh chapter,
a pathway into your kingdom and the joy of everlasting life,
lived with you and all your people for evermore.
Amen.

89

It's incredible

The Apostle Paul

Of this gospel I have become a servant according to the gift of God's grace that was given me by the working of his power. Although I am the very least of all the saints, this grace was given to me to bring to the Gentiles the news of the boundless riches of Christ, and to make everyone see what is the plan of the mystery hidden for ages in God who created all things; so that through the Church the wisdom of God in its rich variety might now be made known to the rulers and authorities in the heavenly places. This was in accordance with the eternal purpose that he has carried out in Christ Jesus our Lord, in whom we have access to God in boldness and confidence through faith in him. I pray therefore that you may not lose heart over my sufferings for you; they are your glory.

Ephesians 3:7–13

Meditation

It's incredible,
quite astonishing!
To think that I, Paul,
the man who hated Jesus and everything about him,
should have come to love him so much.
I can still scarcely credit it.
When I look back and remember the man I used to be,
so certain of my own righteousness,
so determined to destroy his name,
I wonder how I ever changed.
But I did,
totally,
not just in incidental details,
not simply in outward allegiance,
but in my heart and soul,
right down to the very core of my being.
It's as though I'm a new person,
created afresh in the image of my Saviour,
my every thought and impulse different from what they used to be.

Not that I'm perfect, don't think I'm claiming that;
I make my mistakes, all too often,
sometimes despairing of ever being the person I would truly like to be.
Yet even then, at my lowest ebb,
when I fail and fail again,
I know he is with me,
making me whole once more.
I'd have laughed at that once,
greeted the idea with scorn
and poured out more of my poison.
But then I met him,
there on the Damascus road,
and my life was turned upside down.
He called me to be an apostle,
an ambassador in his service,
and though I count myself the least of those who bear that name,
it is my greatest joy
and highest honour.
Not that it's been plain sailing, mind you –
I bear my scars and wear these chains.
And though I've done a lot, thanks to him,
more than I could have imagined possible –
building up his Church,
advancing his kingdom –
I know deep down I've barely started,
still so many yet to reach.
So I press on with one goal in mind –
to serve him more truly,
love him more deeply
and know him more fully,
until the day dawns when I shall see and know him completely,
face to face,
one to one.

Prayer

Loving God,
thank you for your call to discipleship and service –
to sharing in the work of your kingdom.
Thank you for calling us as we are,
with all our faults, weaknesses and doubts,

accepting us not through our own deserving,
but through your grace.
Above all, thank you for working deep within
to change our lives and draw us ever closer to you.
Amen.

Jesus transfigured

90

We saw him that day as never before

The Apostle James

Six days later, Jesus took with him Peter and James and his brother John and led them up a high mountain, by themselves. And he was transfigured before them, and his face shone like the sun, and his clothes became dazzling white . . . suddenly a bright cloud overshadowed them, and from the cloud a voice said, 'This is my Son, the Beloved; with him I am well pleased; listen to him!'

Matthew 17:1, 2, 5b

Meditation

We saw him that day as never before,
literally, in a new light,
glimpsing for the first time just who and what he was.
He'd simply been one of *us* until then,
special, yes,
amazing even,
but essentially a friend,
a teacher,
a person like you and me.
Yet up there on the mountaintop all that changed,
for there was more –
much more –
our eyes opened to new horizons,
the awesome, astonishing truth.
Don't ask for details –
it's all a blur –
but one moment we were catching our breath from the climb
and the next gasping in wonder;
one moment passing the time of day
and the next prostrate in worship,
for suddenly he was transformed before us,
his clothes white as white,
his face radiant,

the world bathed in light.
It was like a divine Yes,
as though everything had been leading up to that moment,
and as if to confirm it, Moses and Elijah appeared by his side,
the bringer of the Law and greatest of the prophets
joining in joyful welcome.
The moment passed, of course, as all do,
and after the heights of the mountain came the depths of the valley,
descent into the shadow of death.
But though darkness came and night fell
through a kiss, a cross and a tomb,
we looked forward in faith to the dawn,
for we had seen God's glory,
the shining of his Son,
light that would rise again.

Prayer

Lord Jesus Christ,
we delight in the fact that you walked on our earth,
sharing our humanity,
being one with us,
but we can forget sometimes that,
just as you were with God in the beginning
so you are with him now,
enthroned on high,
and that, throughout your life and ministry, you made him known,
revealing his wonder and glory to all who had eyes to see
and ears to hear.
Save us from ever reducing the divine to our level,
such that our worship becomes cosy, comfortable and complacent.
Help us, instead, to discern the splendour of the Godhead,
the awesomeness of who and what you are,
and thus to come before you in awe and reverence,
rejoicing at the privilege of entering your presence,
receiving your love
and sharing your life.
Amen.

91

It was fantastic

The Apostle John

Six days later, Jesus took with him Peter and James and John, and led them up a high mountain apart, by themselves. And he was transfigured before them, and his clothes became dazzling white, such as no one on earth could bleach them. And there appeared to them Elijah with Moses, who were talking with Jesus. Then Peter said to Jesus, 'Rabbi, it is good for us to be here; let us make three dwellings, one for you, one for Moses, and one for Elijah.'

Mark 9:2–5

Meditation

It was fantastic,
extraordinary,
mind-blowing;
a once-in-a-lifetime experience,
and I was lucky enough to be there –
me, Peter and James up on the mountain with Jesus.
We knew something was going to happen –
we could see it from his manner when he asked us to join him –
but we never dreamt of anything like that.
He seemed to change before our eyes,
his clothes to glow,
his face to shine.
And then – would you believe it –
who did we see with him but Moses and Elijah!
Clear as day they were,
chatting together like old friends.
We were struck dumb for a moment,
lost for words,
and then dear old Peter got stuck in as usual,
asking if he could make them comfortable,
even perhaps help set up camp.
And why not?

I mean, we were enjoying ourselves,
didn't want the moment to end,
for it was almost too good to be true!
But strangely, as soon as Peter finished speaking,
the spell seemed to break.
The sky darkened as clouds came over
and then, as a peal of thunder broke the silence,
Moses and Elijah disappeared,
leaving Jesus standing there alone,
looking just as he always had,
as ordinary as you or me.
Did we imagine it?
We've often asked ourselves that.
Or was it a vision,
brought on perhaps by the heat or altitude
or simply having had one too many before we set off?
It must have been something like that, surely;
there's no other logical explanation.
Yet it's funny how we all saw the same thing,
all down to the last detail.
I don't know what to make of it,
but I wouldn't have missed it for the world.
It helped me understand what Peter had already begun to grasp:
that Jesus was the Messiah,
the answer to all our prayers,
the fulfilment of the Law and the prophets.
It was just a glimpse,
a moment's wonderful insight which, at the time,
could never be repeated.
And, in a sense, that was true,
for no one will ever witness quite what we saw in the way we saw it.
But others have seen his glory now,
not just the three of us, but his followers everywhere –
the glory of the Father revealed in him,
day after day after day,
full of grace and truth,
And, believe me, that too is fantastic,
extraordinary,
unforgettable!

Prayer

Lord Jesus Christ,
you became flesh,
walking our earth,
sharing our humanity,
identifying yourself with each one of us.
We praise you for that truth,
but save us from allowing it to make us over-familiar,
believing we know all there is to know about you.
Help us always to keep a sense of awe and wonder in worship,
recognising that we are privileged to glimpse in you
the majesty and greatness of God.
Amen.

92

We thought we knew him

The Apostle James

Now Peter and his companions were weighed down with sleep; but since they had stayed awake, they saw his glory and the two men who stood with him. Just as they were leaving him, Peter said to Jesus, 'Master, it is good for us to be here; let us make three dwellings, one for you, one for Moses, and one for Elijah' – not knowing what he said. While he was saying this, a cloud came and overshadowed them; and they were terrified as they entered the cloud. Then from the cloud came a voice that said, 'This is my Son, my Chosen; listen to him!'

Luke 9:32–35

Meditation

We thought we knew him,
that we understood who he was and what he'd come to do.
We'd followed him for months, remember,
walked and talked with him like no other,
so all of us, in our own way, understood he was special,
chosen and called by God.
We believed he was the Messiah, come to set us free –
the one sent by God to establish his kingdom here on earth,
a glorious new beginning.
Never mind the whys and wherefores –
they could wait.
He was here among us,
working out his purpose,
and that was enough.
But we *didn't* really know, after all,
as that day on the mountaintop made clear,
our horizons exposed there as painfully small,
altogether lacking.
For in those extraordinary few moments
we glimpsed him as never before:
bathed in the glory of God,

transformed,
radiant,
not of this world.
And, as if to confirm how unique he was,
a voice came from heaven:
'This is my Son . . .
listen to him.'
We realised then that he didn't just *speak* of God –
he *was* God,
greater than we'd begun to imagine,
than words can ever express,
the cloud that overshadowed us a reminder that we saw but in part,
gazed upon a mighty and marvellous mystery.
We had much to learn,
and we're learning still,
day after day discovering more of his grace,
his love,
his truth.
Never forget the lesson we were given:
that whatever we know of who and what he is,
there will always be far, far more beyond us.

Prayer

Lord Jesus Christ,
we think we know you,
imagine we have understood who and what you are,
but in reality we have barely glimpsed your glory,
scarcely begun to grasp the extent of your power,
scope of your purpose,
breadth of your love
or depth of your mercy.
Remind us that true faith is always growing,
never the finished article;
that we have more to learn,
more to discover,
more to experience of your grace and goodness.
Help to recognise a little more of your greatness each day,
until we finally see and know you in full,
even as we are fully known.
Amen.

93

I wanted to hold on to that moment for ever

Peter

Now about eight days after these sayings Jesus took with him Peter and John and James, and went up on the mountain to pray. And while he was praying, the appearance of his face changed, and his clothes became dazzling white. Suddenly they saw two men, Moses and Elijah, talking to him. They appeared in glory and were speaking of his departure, which he was about to accomplish at Jerusalem.

Luke 9:28–31

Meditation

I wanted to hold on to that moment for ever,
to keep things just as they were for the rest of eternity,
for I feared life would never be so special again.
It was just the four of us –
well, six if you count Moses and Elijah –
the four of us sharing a blessed moment of peace and quiet;
no crowds pleading for a miracle,
lepers begging for healing,
Pharisees baying for his blood,
or Sadducees spoiling for a fight.
Just us,
together,
as we'd all too rarely been.
And we knew it couldn't last;
he'd made that perfectly clear when I dared suggest otherwise.
There was trouble round the corner,
his enemies waiting to pounce,
and we knew it was only a matter of time before they got him.
Not much of a prospect, was it –
rejection, suffering, death?
I don't know how he stuck it, I really don't.
But we didn't want to think about such things,

not then anyway,
and up there on the mountain it all seemed a million miles away,
out of sight, out of mind.
Can you blame me for wanting to stay,
for wanting to hang on to the moment for as long as possible?
Only I couldn't, of course.
Life goes on, as they say,
and you have to go with it,
like it or not.
It was hard to accept that,
hard to go back to the daily round
with its familiar demands and expectations.
Yet as I spoke to Jesus, coming down the mountain,
I realised suddenly it had to be;
that there was no other way –
going back, I mean.
He knew that,
and slowly, very slowly, I came to know it too.
It was a vital time, up there on the mountain –
a special time that gave him new strength,
new resolve,
the inspiration he needed to face the future and fulfil his destiny.
But it was as much for us as for him;
a moment we could look back on
so that afterwards we might keep on looking forward.

Prayer

Loving God,
there are some moments we never want to end,
when we wish we could keep things as they are for ever.
But life is not like that, and neither is faith.
It must always move on if it is to grow,
always develop if it is not to become stale.
Open our hearts then, through Christ, to new experiences of your love
and new insights into your greatness,
so that may we know you a little more fully each day.
Amen.

94

What happened that day up on the mountain?

The Apostle John

Then a cloud overshadowed them, and from the cloud there came a voice, 'This is my Son, the Beloved; listen to him!' Suddenly when they looked around, they saw no one with them any more, but only Jesus.

Mark 9:7, 8

Meditation

What happened that day up on the mountain?
I'm still not sure, even now.
Maybe it was the altitude addling the brain
or perhaps the light playing tricks,
but one moment we seemed to be looking at Jesus –
and the next it was as though he were God himself,
his face radiant,
his clothes dazzling white,
his whole being bathed in light, too bright to behold.
And that's not all,
for there beside him stood Moses and Elijah,
epitomising the Law and prophets,
as though everything that had gone before –
our life, our faith, our history –
had been leading up to that moment,
finding fulfilment in our friend standing there before us.
We didn't grasp all that at first, of course;
in fact we didn't grasp much –
just stood there gawping,
awestruck,
until I blurted out some nonsense about building shelters for them all –
but we realised afterwards we'd been granted a glimpse of glory,
a sign that this man who we loved and followed
was more special than we'd begun to imagine –

too special for words.
We wanted to stay there for ever,
to keep hold of that mountaintop experience,
but life's not like that, sadly.
Like faith, it must be lived out in the daily routine,
in this world of ups and downs,
highs and lows,
and, believe me, we were to have both of those aplenty.
But whatever the trials we were later to face –
the depths of despair, suffering and human evil –
there was no way those could have the final word.
We'd seen the light that day –
literally –
and it would never be extinguished.

Prayer

Lord Jesus Christ,
we think we have grasped the wonder of who and what you are . . .
but we haven't.
We think we understand the extent of your love . . .
but we don't.
We think we can fathom the breadth of your power and goodness . . .
but we can't.
Teach us that there is always more to be revealed of your truth,
more to learn of your mercy,
and more to discover of your purpose,
your glory being far beyond anything we can fully comprehend.
Give us a greater sense of your greatness,
a fuller awareness of all you have done, are doing and continue to do,
and keep us open each day to fresh insights,
new horizons
and deeper experiences of your unsurpassable grace.
Amen.

Mothering Sunday

95

We'd done our best for him

Mary, mother of Jesus

And the child's father and mother were amazed at what was being said about him. Then Simeon blessed them and said to his mother Mary, 'This child is destined for the falling and the rising of many in Israel, and to be a sign that will be opposed so that the inner thoughts of many will be revealed – and a sword will pierce your own soul too.'

Luke 2:33–35

Meanwhile, standing near the cross of Jesus were his mother, and his mother's sister, Mary the wife of Clopas, and Mary Magdalene. When Jesus saw his mother and the disciple whom he loved standing beside her, he said to his mother, 'Woman, here is your son.' Then he said to the disciple, 'Here is your mother.' And from that hour the disciple took her into his own home.

John 19:25–27

Meditation

We'd done our best for him,
packing straw into the manger to make it as soft and safe as possible.
But if I thought I could protect Jesus from danger,
such confidence was swiftly to be questioned,
those words of Simeon's about a sword piercing my soul
sending a chill up my spine.
And, as if to reinforce the threat,
soon afterwards we had to rush off to Egypt,
in fear for our lives from Herod.
Afterwards though, I dared to dream again,
for we enjoyed years of happiness together in Nazareth,
just another family quietly going about our business.
I still worried of course –
mums always do, don't they? –
but it was only after he began preaching and teaching,
healing the sick,

restoring the broken,
proclaiming the kingdom of God,
that my fears resurfaced.
Many followed him,
loving Jesus just as I did,
but inevitably he ruffled feathers,
many others not liking what they heard.
He challenged so much they held dear,
not just questioning the status quo
but threatening to sweep it away altogether.
No surprise, then, that the scribes and Pharisees resolved to silence him,
and eventually seized their chance.
I watched bereft as they nailed him to that cross;
blood seeping from his head, his hands and his feet.
And as he hung there,
convulsed by the pain,
I shared his agony,
my heart broken as only a mother's can be.
I wanted to reach out to hold, protect and comfort.
And when he finally spoke,
entrusting me into the care of his most trusted friend,
I realised he wanted to do precisely the same for me.
I held a special place in his heart,
understandably,
but I'm not the only one.
You do, too,
every one of you.
In the awfulness of his suffering,
his concern was still to love –
to bring healing through his brokenness,
life through his death.
I'd done my best for him;
now he was doing *his* best,
not just for me,
but for all.

Prayer

Lord Jesus Christ,
thank you that though we deserve it so little
you love us so much;
that you value each of us infinitely,
enough to die for.
Thank you for staying true to your chosen path,
despite the hostility you faced,
the misunderstanding you endured,
the pain you suffered
and the darkness you confronted.
In the ugliness that scars the beauty of this world,
the shadow of evil, hatred and death,
teach us that your light shines through
and your love will triumph,
life, now and for all eternity, being held safely in your hands.
Amen.

96

I was so proud

Mary, mother of Jesus

And the child's father and mother were amazed at what was being said about him. Then Simeon blessed them and said to his mother Mary, 'This child is destined for the falling and the rising of many in Israel, and to be a sign that will be opposed so that the inner thoughts of many will be revealed – and a sword will pierce your own soul too.'

Luke 2:33–35

Meanwhile, standing near the cross of Jesus were his mother, and his mother's sister, Mary the wife of Clopas, and Mary Magdalene. When Jesus saw his mother and the disciple whom he loved standing beside her, he said to his mother, 'Woman, here is your son.' Then he said to the disciple, 'Here is your mother.' And from that hour the disciple took her into his own home.

John 19:25–27

Meditation

I was so proud,
so happy as I held our child close,
cradling him in my arms.
He seemed more special,
more precious,
than I'd dreamt possible,
and I wept tears of joy.
But just days later,
a shadow fell that was never quite to lift,
for that man Simeon, as we took Jesus to the Temple,
warned of hurt,
heartbreak,
a sword piercing my soul.
And now, all this time later,
after years of wondering,
hoping he might be wrong,

I've come, all too clearly, to see what he meant.
For it's my boy up there, hanging on that cross;
it's my boy, grimacing with pain;
it's my boy, broken and bleeding;
it's my boy, breathing his last –
and no words can express my pain.
He brought it on himself, in a sense,
choosing the way of the cross,
and though I'd begged him to think again,
I'd known all along, in my heart of hearts,
that there was no other way –
that he had to fulfil his calling.
My heart ached with pride,
even while it groaned with grief,
and, if earlier, joy had been touched with sorrow,
now sorrow was touched with joy,
for even as he writhed there in agony,
he looked down at me
and showed how much he cared,
asking John,
his dearest, closest friend,
to look after me –
treat me like a mum.
I had to let go of my child –
we all do, don't we? –
his life having brought me both pleasure and pain,
laughter and tears.
But, whatever the cost, it was worth it,
a thousand times over,
for through him, I've been truly blessed,
and so also, if you've only eyes to see it, have *you*.

Prayer

For the wonder of your love, Lord,
poured out for many;
for the immensity of your sacrifice,
offered for all;
for the depth of your care,
never exhausted;
for the richness of your blessing,
so freely given;
from the bottom of our hearts, we thank you.
Amen.

97

Why me?

Mary, mother of Jesus

The angel said to her, 'Do not be afraid, Mary, for you have found favour with God. And now, you will conceive in your womb and bear a son, and you will name him Jesus. He will be great, and will be called the Son of the Most High, and the Lord God will give to him the throne of his ancestor David. He will reign over the house of Jacob for ever, and of his kingdom there will be no end.'

Luke 1:30–33

Meanwhile, standing near the cross of Jesus were his mother, and his mother's sister, Mary the wife of Clopas, and Mary Magdalene. When Jesus saw his mother and the disciple whom he loved standing beside her, he said to his mother, 'Woman, here is your son.' Then he said to the disciple, 'Here is your mother.' And from that hour the disciple took her into his own home.

John 19:25–27

Meditation

Why me?
That's what I kept on asking myself.
Why me?
I mean, it was obvious what people were going to say, wasn't it?
The sly looks,
the knowing grins,
the wagging tongues.
And Joseph?
Well, he really hit the roof.
Furious he was, and who can blame him?
If we'd been married it would have been different,
but engaged – it was bound to cause a scandal.
And it hurt, more than anyone will know;
I never realised people could be so cruel.
I didn't even want a baby, that's what made it worse;

it was the last thing on my mind.
I was still young,
not ready for that kind of responsibility,
wanting to enjoy life a little.
I could have done without those sleepless nights,
the endless washing,
the countless extra demands.
And believe me, it didn't get any easier.
Well, it never does, does it?
I'll never forget how he disappeared like that
on the way back from Jerusalem –
a right old panic he had us in.
But was he sorry?
Well, if he was he had a funny way of showing it.
'You should have known where to find me,' he said.
'My Father's house, where else?'
Cheeky monkey!
And then, just when life was plodding along nicely,
back on an even keel,
he went swanning off into the wilderness to be baptised.
Oh, I know he had to make his own way, don't get me wrong,
but I couldn't help feeling he was getting mixed up
in something dangerous.
And so it proved.
We could all see it coming,
all except *him* apparently.
He said the wrong things
to the wrong people
in the wrong places,
and there could only be one result.
It nearly broke my heart to watch it –
my beautiful boy, broken and bleeding,
struggling with that cross,
hanging in agony.
But then he looked down,
not at the rest of them
but at me.
And in his eyes was such love,
such care,
such tenderness!
I saw suddenly the eyes of God looking at me

through the eyes of my child,
and I asked myself then,
as I'd asked so many times before,
yet differently this time,
so very differently:
why me?
Why *me*?

Prayer

Loving God, sometimes we cannot help but ask 'why?'
Why me?
Why this?
Why anything?
There is so much we do not understand,
so much that apparently contradicts our faith,
leaving us groping for answers.
And we feel guilty about having such questions,
afraid that somehow we are letting the side down
through entertaining them.
Yet in our hearts we know there is no point pretending,
for we can never deceive you.
So help us rather to admit there are things we cannot make sense of,
and to trust that though *we* may never understand,
you do.
Amen.

98

I could have brained those children

Andrew

People were bringing even infants to him that he might touch them; and when the disciples saw it, they sternly ordered them not to do it. But Jesus called for them and said, 'Let the little children come to me, and do not stop them; for it is to such as these that the kingdom of God belongs. Truly I tell you, whoever does not receive the kingdom of God as a little child will never enter it.'

Luke 18:15–17

Meditation

I could have brained those children,
rushing around like that with their yelling and shrieking,
shattering our peace and quiet.
We'd had him alone at last,
just us and Jesus;
a rare opportunity to sit and listen undisturbed,
drinking in his every word.
And it was wonderful,
a truly magical moment,
until, that is, *they* turned up –
those wretched kids ushered forward by their doting parents,
just so that he could touch them.
Honestly, how ridiculous!
Superstition, that's all it was –
no real faith behind any of it –
just sentimental rubbish,
nauseating!
So we tried to stop them; you can understand that, surely?
We wanted to get back to the business in hand
before we were so rudely interrupted;
back to more serious matters.
Okay, so maybe we were a bit over the top,
a touch more heavy than the situation demanded,

but we were angry,
disappointed.
I mean, could *you* have concentrated with that row going on?
I couldn't.
Yet did they care?
Not likely!
We fully expected Jesus to back us up,
send the lot of them packing.
But can you believe this? He didn't!
He actually turned on us,
and there was anger in his eyes,
anger touched almost with pity.
'Leave them alone,' he said.
'Let them come to me.
What's your problem?'
Well, we didn't know what to say, did we?
It caught us right on the hop.
So we just fidgeted uncomfortably,
trying to cover our embarrassment.
It was so unfair.
We'd meant no harm, after all,
certainly hadn't meant to upset anybody;
yet there they were now,
the kids bawling their eyes out,
the mums looking daggers at us,
the dads having a go at everyone –
what a mess!
I truly didn't know what to do next.
But thankfully Jesus came to the rescue as always.
He reached out and took the children in his arms, one by one,
enfolding them in a great loving hug.
And then he lifted them up for all to see.
'These are special,' he told us,
'More precious than you will ever know –
each one treasured by God.'
And you could tell from the way he smiled at them,
and the way they smiled back at him,
that he meant every word he was saying,
and that they knew he meant it.
I still feel a bit aggrieved by it all –
well, you can tell that, can't you?

But I realise now we made ourselves look rather silly that day,
even childish, you might say;
and I'm beginning to understand Jesus has no room for the childish,
only the child*like*.

Prayer

Lord Jesus Christ,
you told your disciples that the kingdom of heaven
belongs to little children;
that unless we become like them
we shall not enter it ourselves.
Teach us what that means.
Help us to be truly childlike in our faith,
having a child's innocence,
a child's hunger to learn,
and a child's total trust.
Help us, like them, to step out gladly into the great adventure of faith.
Amen.

99

I was scared at first

One of the little children

Then little children were being brought to him in order that he might lay his hands on them and pray. The disciples spoke sternly to those who brought them; but Jesus said, 'Let the little children come to me, and do not stop them; for it is to such as these that the kingdom of heaven belongs.' And he laid his hands on them and went on his way.

Matthew 19:13–15

Meditation

I was scared at first,
scared of the noise, the crowds, the confusion –
a sea of faces unlike anything I'd seen before.
It seemed that everyone wanted to see Jesus –
everyone, that is, except us;
we just wanted to get back to our friends
and enjoy ourselves as we'd been doing before.
Who was he anyway, that's what we wanted to know?
What made him so special, so important?
Yet it was no use arguing,
one look at my mother's face told me that –
she was determined I was going to see him, like it or not.
So there we were, pushing through the crowd,
her hand clasping mine
in case I should have any ideas about escaping –
and slowly fear turned to rebellion.
Okay, I'd go if I had to,
but if she expected me to be sweetness and light
she could think again.
I resolved instead to give Jesus an audience he'd never forget,
to scowl, sulk, scream the place down if I had to –
anything to make clear whose idea this daft business was.
Yet that's not the way it worked out.
I had the scowl ready all right,

a sullen snarl to be proud of,
but the moment I saw him it just melted away,
all hostility and resentment forgotten.
I can't tell you why exactly,
but there was something quite extraordinary about him,
an interest, warmth and concern that seemed to flow over you,
impossible to resist.
Instead of treating us like kids he made us feel important,
as though we were worth something to him,
special –
and suddenly, instead of sulking,
we were beaming with sheer delight,
even, would you believe, when he picked us up
and started to pray for us.
There's not many I'd have let do that, I can tell you!
He was so different from those followers of his –
you could tell they were itching to get rid of us,
their annoyance at our intrusion all too clear.
Yet do you know what Jesus said to them?
That the kingdom of God belongs to children like us!
I can't think why, for we were no angels, not by a long way,
and I can't imagine he was under any illusions –
presumably he saw something in us we didn't.
I tell you what, though –
we'd have followed him anywhere after that,
walked to the ends of the earth and back had he asked us.
No, we didn't understand quite who he was
or what he'd come to do –
but that didn't matter –
we knew instinctively that he was someone special,
a man we could trust completely,
with our very lives if necessary,
and that was enough.
What more could we have wanted?
What more could anyone ask?

Prayer

Gracious God,
we thank you for the great adventure of life
in all its endless diversity and richness.
We thank you that, whoever we are,
there is always more to learn,
more to explore and more to experience.
Keep our minds open to that special truth for,
as the years pass,
we can lose our sense of childlike wonder and fascination,
becoming worldly-wise or blasé about life,
taking for granted those things that once stirred our imagination,
and sinking into an ever-deeper rut of cynicism and over-familiarity.
Help us to recapture the innocence and spontaneity
of our childhood years;
the ability to look at the world with open eyes,
to trust in the future and to celebrate the present.
Give us faith in life,
and in you.
Amen.

100

He took our children in his arms

Those who brought their children to Jesus

People were bringing little children to him in order that he might touch them; and the disciples spoke sternly to them. But when Jesus saw this, he was indignant and said to them, 'Let the little children come to me; do not stop them; for it is to such as these that the kingdom of God belongs. Truly I tell you, whoever does not receive the kingdom of God as a little child will never enter it.'

Mark 10:13–15

Meditation

1 He took our children in his arms,
welcoming them with a smile on his lips
and warmth in his eyes,
but had it been up to those disciples of his,
none of us would have got anywhere near him,
for they brusquely shooed us away.

2 Don't distract him, was the message.
Can't you see the Master's busy;
that he's got better things to do with his time than fritter it away
on doting mothers and their soppy kids?

3 And, were it not for Jesus, we'd have gone home,
disappointed,
angry,
but resigned.

1 He, though, was more indignant than *any* of us,
reprimanding his followers as though *they* were the children,
and then he turned to our little ones,
all attention,
as though nothing in the world could matter to him more.

3 And, do you know what? – I actually think that's true.
They were special to *him*, that much was obvious,
but he reckoned also they were special to *God*,
the kingdom of heaven somehow theirs.

2 We were flabbergasted at that,
for we'd a sneaking feeling the disciples were right –
that faith's not kid's stuff,
but difficult,
demanding,
hard to understand.
3 It's not, though.
It's incredibly simple –
about responding to love,
receiving a gift,
accepting a welcome.
1 *We're* the ones who complicate it,
not God.
We burden others with heavy loads
and tie ourselves in knots,
when he longs only to set us free.
2 Don't try to work it out.
Don't get bogged down in the details.
Receive the kingdom, he said, as a little child
or you may never enter it at all.

Prayer

Gracious God,
thank you for accepting us into the family of your people –
for welcoming us, not as slaves or servants,
but as your children,
precious to you.
Teach us what that means,
and help us always to retain a youthful faith,
fresh,
trusting,
enthusiastic –
not childish
but childlike,
full of hope and anticipation.
Give us innocence and humility to accept
that we depend ultimately on you,
and that, however long we've been walking the way of Christ,
we've still only just begun.
Amen.

Index of Key Themes

Index of Principal Characters

Index of Bible Passages